SpringerBriefs in Education

We are delighted to announce SpringerBriefs in Education, an innovative product type that combines elements of both journals and books. Briefs present concise summaries of cutting-edge research and practical applications in education. Featuring compact volumes of 50 to 125 pages, the SpringerBriefs in Education allow authors to present their ideas and readers to absorb them with a minimal time investment. Briefs are published as part of Springer's eBook Collection. In addition, Briefs are available for individual print and electronic purchase.

SpringerBriefs in Education cover a broad range of educational fields such as: Science Education, Higher Education, Educational Psychology, Assessment & Evaluation, Language Education, Mathematics Education, Educational Technology, Medical Education and Educational Policy.

SpringerBriefs typically offer an outlet for:

- An introduction to a (sub)field in education summarizing and giving an overview of theories, issues, core concepts and/or key literature in a particular field
- A timely report of state-of-the art analytical techniques and instruments in the field of educational research
- A presentation of core educational concepts
- An overview of a testing and evaluation method
- A snapshot of a hot or emerging topic or policy change
- An in-depth case study
- A literature review
- A report/review study of a survey
- An elaborated thesis

Both solicited and unsolicited manuscripts are considered for publication in the SpringerBriefs in Education series. Potential authors are warmly invited to complete and submit the Briefs Author Proposal form. All projects will be submitted to editorial review by editorial advisors.

SpringerBriefs are characterized by expedited production schedules with the aim for publication 8 to 12 weeks after acceptance and fast, global electronic dissemination through our online platform SpringerLink. The standard concise author contracts guarantee that:

- an individual ISBN is assigned to each manuscript
- each manuscript is copyrighted in the name of the author
- the author retains the right to post the pre-publication version on his/her website or that of his/her institution

More information about this series at http://www.springer.com/series/8914

Hyejin Kim

How Global Capital is Remaking International Education

The Emergence of Transnational Education Corporations

Springer

Hyejin Kim
Faculty of Arts and Social Sciences
National University of Singapore
Singapore, Singapore

ISSN 2211-1921   ISSN 2211-193X   (electronic)
SpringerBriefs in Education
ISBN 978-981-32-9671-8   ISBN 978-981-32-9672-5   (eBook)
https://doi.org/10.1007/978-981-32-9672-5

© The Author(s), under exclusive license to Springer Nature Singapore Pte Ltd., part of Springer Nature 2019
This work is subject to copyright. All rights are reserved by the Publisher, whether the whole or part of the material is concerned, specifically the rights of translation, reprinting, reuse of illustrations, recitation, broadcasting, reproduction on microfilms or in any other physical way, and transmission or information storage and retrieval, electronic adaptation, computer software, or by similar or dissimilar methodology now known or hereafter developed.
The use of general descriptive names, registered names, trademarks, service marks, etc. in this publication does not imply, even in the absence of a specific statement, that such names are exempt from the relevant protective laws and regulations and therefore free for general use.
The publisher, the authors and the editors are safe to assume that the advice and information in this book are believed to be true and accurate at the date of publication. Neither the publisher nor the authors or the editors give a warranty, expressed or implied, with respect to the material contained herein or for any errors or omissions that may have been made. The publisher remains neutral with regard to jurisdictional claims in published maps and institutional affiliations.

This Springer imprint is published by the registered company Springer Nature Singapore Pte Ltd.
The registered company address is: 152 Beach Road, #21-01/04 Gateway East, Singapore 189721, Singapore

For my son, who teaches me more than any teacher I have met, and for my husband, who made me realize how education and life go together.

Preface

In the past decade, transnational education corporations have burst onto the private schooling scene. Private firms, publicly listed firms, and private equity groups have transformed international education into an industry valued at over USD 30 billion. Nowhere is the impact stronger and more sudden than in Asia. The top three international school firms with a presence in Asia run more than 20 schools in East and Southeast Asia with another six in India. Ten years ago they had none. Each educates tens of thousands of students around the world and earns annual revenue over USD 300 million. The quiet rise of transnational education corporations—or TECs—has implications for education systems around the world, as private interests gain a greater stake in the future of how schools operate. We need to understand who these firms are, how they have grown, and what they do.

Privately financed education has been a major topic in national debates about education, especially in the United Kingdom and the United states. A study of international schools may seem peripheral to those concerns. After all, these are fee-charging schools that enroll mostly the children of high-income expatriates outside of public education systems. The primary and secondary schools in East and Southeast Asia that are the focus of this book educate only a small percentage of the region's children. These schools do not feature prominently in public debates about education. This invisibility, though, is precisely cause for concern. Corporatization and transnationalization of international schools have meant a spatial division between investors and financial beneficiaries, on one hand, and those directly affected, on the other. The overseas operations of a UK-based edu-business will not gain much attention in education debates in Britain, nor does the fact that education reforms in that country helped spawn firms that later went global. At the same time, foreign acquisition of elite international schools may seem peripheral to public concerns in, say, Cambodia or Vietnam. Globalization in many fields works precisely through these divisions. Without arousing controversy, TECs have grown. Now, having swelled in stature, the largest are assuming public profiles and subtly raising challenges to public education in Asia.

Chapter 1 introduces the subject and its significance. In Chap. 2, "The Creation of an International Education Sector," I give an overview of the transformation of international schooling from an area of education to a business activity. It is now common to describe education as a "sector." This vocabulary makes it easy to forget that education is not necessarily a sector. The international school landscape has only very recently become a sector, and it is a specific set of actors that have propelled that change.

In Chap. 3, "The Origins of International School Groups," I introduce three sets of forces that have contributed to the making of transnational edu-businesses specializing in international schools. One is a supply-side factor: "school choice" reforms in the West, especially in the UK, fostered for-profit school operators who have since gone global. This far-reaching effect of Western education reforms deserves attention. Another factor is demand-side: rising wealth in Asia, plus particular approaches to achieving social mobility, have helped companies create a customer base. A final factor might be called logistical: the de-nationalization of education enables firms to offer a product that makes sense in multiple cultural contexts.

The next two chapters focus on the role of the state in making space for corporatized international schools. Chapter 4, "Government Policies and the Shifting Place of International Schools in the Education System," situates international school policy in a wider context. Here I argue that policies on international schools are fundamental to the integrity of public education systems. Because policies on international schools address issues such as student eligibility for enrolment, these policies guard the boundary around public education systems. I show how several states in Asia have grappled with the problem of whether to allow more children to opt out of public and national education systems in favor of international schools. While governments respond differently, none have prevented the protections on the education system from being breached by international schools.

Chapter 5, "Economic Planning, Education Policy, and International Schools," places international school policy in the context of economic planning. States have actively promoted corporatization and globalization of international schools. For purposes of making the national economy competitive against other countries, states have encouraged the development of the international school business. Drives to attract foreign business and to develop "knowledge economies" have led states to take actions that welcome edu-businesses for international schools.

In Chap. 6, "The Business of International Education," I turn squarely to the operation of TECs. I outline the reasons that make international schools attractive for investment, as well as the ownership structures of prominent firms in this area. I describe pathways from other business areas, such as from other fields of education or from property development, into international schools. I introduce strategies for expansion as well as marketing activities. In all these areas, I argue, the corporatized organization encourages schools to devote more resources and energy to business than to educating young people. The point is not that results for children are poor, but rather that educating becomes a secondary focus to primary revenue-generating tasks.

Chapter 7, "International Education Goes Global: Transnational Education Corporations as Global Actors," offers a closer look at how edu-businesses have an impact on a "global" scale. I show that these businesses have appropriated the notion of "global" for themselves. Corporate understandings inform the idea of global education that they embrace. Edu-businesses present global schools as ones that are similar in different parts of the world, just as a coffee chain might present its product. These meanings of global—for which alternatives could be imagined—form the basis for the ideas that TECs propagate in global forums. I show how the most prominent international school operators are tied up in wider dialogues about education. These occur at events such as the World Economic Forum, through charities and links to major philanthropic initiatives, and with international institutions such as the United Nations and the World Bank. In other words, international school operators are increasingly influential in shaping public, global discussions of education.

While this book is based on social scientific research, it is also shaped by my background working in international school management. I worked for 4 years for a government-supported international school in Singapore. In the positions I held there, finally as managing director, I observed first-hand many aspects of the operations of international schools. Moreover, my period with the school, from 2007 to 2010, coincided with a period of rapid change. Foreign firms were acquiring international schools. Existing ones were expanding and rolling out luxury facilities. Programs like International Baccalaureate (IB) were just starting to become known by parents. Potential buyers were circling around rising schools. That moment was foundational to the creation of an international school sector. I gained further insight into this field when I was recruited to join one of the largest TECs. Working in admissions and marketing, I witnessed from the inside how the firm operated. I stayed with the company for nearly a year before resuming my academic career. Most of the material presented in this book does not come directly from my experiences, but I am able to verify, or triangulate, findings from the material I have gathered with what I learned through direct experience.

My experience also made me think that the subject of international school corporatization and globalization is one deserving greater attention. My concerns about the implications of trends in this field for public education systems, for inequality, and for social solidarity prompted me to look more closely at this subject. I have prepared this book with three sets of audiences in mind. First, I have written it for specialists in comparative education, particularly those who study education management and policy. The book complements existing research on education's globalization and corporatization. Second, social scientists who are interested in globalization can read the book as a study of a lesser known field of globalization. The book adds to the critiques of neoliberalism. Third, I have written the book for nonspecialists who are concerned about the future of education. This book offers an introduction to a set of organizations that may feel remote to most readers, but that can have implications for us collectively.

Singapore
April 2019

Hyejin Kim

Contents

1 Introduction 1
  Why Study International School Operators? 1
  International Education and Elite Schools 2
  The Global Education Industry 4
  Neoliberal Globalization and the International School Industry 6
  Modes of Change in the International School Landscape 7
    State Policies Weaken State Regulatory Capacities 7
    International Schools Become Side-Businesses
    for Other Investments 8
    Internationalization Becomes Co-Opted by Corporate Forces 9
    Consumer Cultures of Education Deflect Critical Engagement 10
  Scope and Approach 11
  References 12

2 The Creation of an International Education Sector 15
  Traditional International Schools 16
  The Creation of an International Education Sector 17
    Competition 17
    Building "Global" Identities 18
    Growing the Market: Recruiting Local Students 19
    Entrance of School Corporations 20
  The Shifting International Education Landscape in Singapore 22
  Conclusion 26
  References 26

3 The Origins of International School Groups 29
  International Schools and the Global Education Industry 30
    Education Reforms and the Rise of Education Firms 31
    De-nationalization as a Force for Edu-Business Entry into
    International Education 37

Demand in Asia for International Schools		38
Conclusion		40
References		41

4 Government Policies and the Shifting Place of International Schools in the Education System 43

Managing Difference and Inequality in Former British Colonies 44
    Malaysia 45
    Singapore....................................... 46
Defining Citizenship and Legitimizing Differences in Democracies 48
    South Korea..................................... 48
    Indonesia 50
Protecting National Identity and Empowering Markets in Post-socialist
Contexts....................................... 51
    Vietnam....................................... 52
    China 53
Conclusion....................................... 55
References 55

5 Economic Planning, Education Policy, and International Schools ... 57

National Economic Competition and International School Growth 58
Promoting International Schools in Order to Compete: Singapore 60
Building a "Knowledge Economy": Malaysia..................... 62
Conclusion....................................... 63
References 64

6 The Business of International Education 67

Why Invest in International Education? 68
Owners of International Schools and Their Interests 70
    From Private Equity to International Education 70
    From Other Types of Education to International Schools 71
    From Property Development to International Schools,
    and Vice Versa 71
    From International Schools to Other Businesses 73
How Do International Education Businesses Grow? 74
    Sources of Expansion 74
    Building Brands? 75
How Do TECs Find Customers? 78
    Demonstrating Prestige............................. 78
    IB and the "Economization" of Education 80
Who Runs Schools? 82
    Circulation of Teachers............................. 82
    School Management 83
Conclusion....................................... 83
References 85

Contents

7 International Education Goes Global: Transnational Education Corporations as Global Actors 87

Global Education Policy Networks 88

The Meanings of a "Global" Education 91

    Global as Homogenizing................................... 91

    Global as Luxury Consumption............................. 93

    Global as Stratifying in New Ways 94

International Education and Policy Networks 96

    The Revolving Door...................................... 96

    Foundations and Charity Work 97

    Global Education Experts 98

    Government Consulting 99

Conclusion 100

References 101

8 Conclusion 103

Making Education Global 103

Implications for Teaching and Learning 104

The State and Education 105

Reference 106

Chapter 1
Introduction

The past fifteen years have seen the expansion of a mode of international schooling that is corporate, favorable to big firms, and increasingly a challenge to state regulation. Where have the providers of this mode of schooling come from? How have they grown so quickly? What consequences can be expected for school systems and patterns of inequality? These are some of the questions answered in this book.

Why Study International School Operators?

International school operators have gained relatively little attention in scholarship on education markets. They can appear as a low priority for research agendas on comparative and international education. Public schooling is not at stake. The students and their families do not belong to a vulnerable population. Only a small percentage of students, largely from privileged backgrounds, attend these international schools. There are, however, good reasons to examine international school operators.

First, international education is a worthy aspiration. All of the schools and firms examined here profess a dedication to instilling international or global sensibilities in young people. This cause is one many would support. How successful have these schools been in developing international education? Are there lessons that can be learned for others seeking to make education more international? A study of international schools can possibly shed light on these questions.

Second, the edu-businesses at the heart of the expansion of international schools are large and growing quickly. They make deals with governments in order to get licenses or gain access to land and, in some cases, subsidies; some even advise governments. Given these ties to public affairs, these increasingly powerful actors need to be better understood. Furthermore, the focus of much education scholarship is on schools, so the role of operators can go missing even in research on international schools.

© The Author(s), under exclusive license to Springer Nature Singapore Pte Ltd., part of Springer Nature 2019
H. Kim, *How Global Capital is Remaking International Education*, SpringerBriefs in Education, https://doi.org/10.1007/978-981-32-9672-5_1

Third, international school operators will have an impact on national education systems. As the boundary between international schools and broader education systems becomes more porous, parents who can afford to may pursue ways of sending their children to international options—either in-country or overseas. There is also the aspirational effect: corporatized international education tends to be celebrated by precisely those who set aspirations for the rest of society. The implications for inequality and social solidarity can be tremendous. If the wealthy and upwardly mobile shift toward international schools, then commitment to public education systems can decline. Furthermore, the rise of transnational education corporations (TECs) signals the emergence of increasingly powerful forces who would support continued marketization of school systems. When in the 1980s and 1990s governments in the United Kingdom, the United States, and Sweden began to undertake "school choice" reforms, pro-business forces were among the biggest proponents but there was no major pre-existing education industry. The situation now is different. The debate is no longer just academic or ideological: there is a massive industry waiting to tap into opportunities to acquire, build, and operate schools.

Fourth, TECs offer a lens onto fundamental processes of globalization. An investigation into the growth of these firms is a case study in neoliberal globalization. Powerful business interests, in cooperation with particular governmental actors, have turned an area of service into an economic sector. Shifts in one corner of the world have contributed to profound changes in another. Through subtle means, new markets have been created. These markets have contributed to demarcating class and status distinctions, and, possibly, reconfiguring those distinctions.

It should be added here that in offering a critical look at international school providers I am not aiming to blame international schools, their staff, or the parents who enroll their children in them, nor am I leveling criticism at the quality of education offered in these schools. Rather, it is important to understand how we got here. Many of the decisions made by individuals appear straightforward—investors seeking a quick turnaround or stable asset growth, teachers traveling the world for enriching experiences, parents looking to give their children a leg up. We can learn more about the emerging social configurations by empathizing with these actors. Parents may even dislike the corporate style and the absence of democratic understandings of education, not to mention the high fees, but the bottom line for most is that they feel international schools can give their children the best start in life. There is little point in judging that assessment. Instead, we need to know how a situation was created in which such schools could be presented as the best option.

International Education and Elite Schools

Any definition of an *international school* can be contested (Bunnell, 2007). A good reason for a lack of academic consensus on what constitutes an international school is that the regulatory environment shapes whether schools take on the "international" label. That label can have a particular legal meaning in one country and a different meaning in another. In identifying the scope of the international school landscape, we should thus be sensitive to these shifting meanings. At the same time, among practitioners there is something much closer to a consensus on what an international school is. Administrators from these schools meet each other at various venues, such as teacher job fairs. Parents also imagine international schools as a clear category, associated in particular with curricula and diplomas that are internationally accredited.

This book deals with self-labeled international schools at the primary and secondary levels. Most such schools offer diplomas or curricula that are recognized beyond the host country, with International Baccalaureate (IB) and Cambridge programs being the most widespread. The corporations I focus on own and operate such schools in multiple countries. Early education is excluded, as is technical training and supplementary education. Unlike primary and secondary education, those fields began as business-created sectors in many places. However, as shall be seen, it is not uncommon for a school operator to also have interests in related education businesses. The operators discussed here, called edu-businesses or TECs, are revenue-oriented organizations. I include operators that hold non-profit status because they can be revenue-oriented and display many of the same characteristics as for-profit firms. Whether operators have for-profit or non-profit status is partly an artifact of jurisdiction-specific rules, and the distinction is not necessarily one separating fundamentally different types of organizations.

The growth of these schools has been especially prominent in Asia. English-language schools have become more desirable to parents who hope their children can attend university in an Anglophone country. According to 2016 ISC research, Asia has shown more growth in students' numbers than other regions between 2011 and 2016. At present, 54% of international schools are present in Asia and 60% students are as well (Independent Education Today, 2016). These international schools are the subject of a growing body of research (see esp. Hayden, Levy, & Thompson, 2015).

A question in this literature is the meaning of "global" or "international" education. Studies point to the necessity of looking beyond stated objectives of schools and curricula to the messages that are transmitted to parents. With echoes of colonialism, international schools can even pedal "Englishness as currency" (Gardner-McTaggart, 2018: 110). Beyond promising not only an English-language education, these schools can intimate that they broker cultural capital. A theme in research on international schools is that—regardless of their missions—they can become primarily oriented to functioning as a means of attaining status. One study, for example, shows that IB coordinators in Asia focus on "instrumentalist functions" when adopting IB's Middle Years Program (MYP) (Wright, Lee, Tang, & Tsui, 2016: 13). Another research argues that IB is mostly used for "elitist social reproduction" (Gardner-McTaggart, 2016: 3). International schools become sites of "social class-making" (Tarc & Tarc, 2014). These trends have raised concerns about students in international schools become disconnected both host and home societies. Borrowing a term from political philosopher Michael Sandel, Lee and Wright (2016: 130–131) warn that the elite tendency in international schools in the region tends toward a "skyboxification of education."

This book contributes to these discussions of international schools. Existing research focuses on teachers and students; less has been presented on school operators. I place the operators at the center. I also bring an insider perspective. While former teachers in international schools have contributed to research in this area, I offer the perspective of a former manager. Because I have worked with international schools in that capacity, I give greater attention to the practical aspects of operating an international school.

The Global Education Industry

A wider field of work that this book may be positioned in concerns education as a business that crosses national borders. In national settings, the corporatization of education has been a major subject of concern and research (Kovacs, 2011; Lubienski, 2005; Saltman, 2005). The "global education industry" comprises a broad range of education and education-related activities. Education is not simply teaching, learning, and socialization; it is now also an economic activity. This industry involves a wide range of institutions, from top secondary schools and university to private tuition firms and test preparation companies, from government agencies to middlemen who specialize in placing international students in schools, and from diploma granting organizations like the International Baccalaureate Organization (IBO) to privately-owned networks of schools (Bunnell, 2007; Sidhu, 2002). Accompanying the emergence of an education industry have been the trappings of the corporate world, such as branding and the widespread use of catchy metaphors to describe education projects (Olds & Robertson, 2008).

The construction of education markets has been a core theme in research on the global education industry. How do education markets get created? What are the implications of global education business actors? Why do internationalization and corporatization tend to go hand in hand? Market creation is increasingly a focus of attention in research on education policy and the education industry (Komljenovic & Robertson, 2017). As markets have emerged in a variety of fields, from testing to textbooks to student recruitment to school operations, the problem of how markets get created takes center stage (Au & Hollar, 2016; Molnar, 2006).

These questions lead to examining linkages between business and government, as government action is necessary to create markets. As Stephen Ball (2009: 97) notes in relation to a range of education policy areas in the United Kingdom, the cause of the emergence of education businesses "is not some kind of spontaneous neo-liberal free market, its dynamics have to be understood alongside the dynamics of and changes in the state itself and the role of the state in shaping industry behavior and economic transactions." Private enterprises, charitable foundations with privatizing missions, inter-governmental organizations like the World Bank, and governmental actors are all involved in the formation of education markets and policies that support those markets (Ball, 2012; Verger, Steiner-Khamsi, & Lubienski, 2017).

The Global Education Industry 5

In the United Kingdom and United States, school reform programs have led to the corporatization and privatization of schooling. Reforms in other areas have also been relevant. For example, revision of the Charities Act in the Britain encouraged elite schools to seek overseas expansion and become revenue-seeking brands (Bunnell, 2009). Meanwhile, in the Asia Pacific, governments have undertaken national projects to make education more international as their economies move toward being based on knowledge creation (Lai & Maclean, 2011; Lewis, 2011; Lui, 2014; Olds, 2007; Sidhu & Kaur, 2011). Singapore and other advanced Asian economies started to shift in the late 1990s toward knowledge-based economies. This shift implied renewed investment in education. These projects have made universities more like corporate entities and have sparked waves of student mobility. Industries surrounding education have grown. These changes have worked to unhinge education systems from simple goals of serving national populations.

Links between government and business on education have led to an emerging scholarly conversation on networks of "global education policy" (Ball 2012; Exley, Brawn, & Ball, 2011). Stephen Ball and other UK-based scholars have pioneered research in this area. As research in this field indicates, private and public actors in education have become woven together on a global scale (Gulson & Lubienski, 2014). Education policy today is entangled in this "heterarchical" web (Olmedo, 2014).

A pillar of the education industry in Asia is the counter-intuitive relationship between public schooling and heavy family investment in children's education. In Asia, parents have been disciplined in the idea that they should pay for education—even when compulsory education is essentially free. Even as public education is free (or inexpensive) and well-attended in places such as South Korea, Japan, Taiwan, Singapore, and Chinese cities, sending children to supplementary and privately-operated after-school programs has become a norm (Entrich, 2018; Kim, 2016; Roesgaard, 2006). This internalization of the idea that one should pay for education—and pay more for better education—helps set the basis for international school expansion.

Student mobility has contributed to the globalization of the education industry. International schools have also become reasons for mobility rather than just consequences of mobile careers. Korean mothers move with their children to Malaysia, Singapore, or the Philippines for international school opportunities (*Chosŏn Ilbo* Jan. 26, 2008; Chew, 2009). There children can gain stronger English skills and diplomas, such as IB and IGCSE, which are legible to university admissions officers in the United States, the United Kingdom, Canada, and Australia.

Verger, Steiner-Khamsi, and Lubienski (2017) identify three forms of the global education industry. These are neoliberal reforms, the globalization of standards, and the propagation of for-profit schools in lower-income societies. None of these strikes to the core of shifts in international school operations. A closer examination of the international school industry can possibly expand understandings of the forms of the global education industry. As businesses that are well-plugged into some of the most lucrative and high-status parts of the education world, international school operators are also crucial actors in the global education industry.

Neoliberal Globalization and the International School Industry

International schools should be placed in an even broader context. The current changes in education, as one set of scholars notes, should be "understood as being embedded within interdependent local, national, and global political economy complexes" (Verger, Steiner-Khamsi, & Lubienski, 2016: 18). The growth of international school operators can be seen as a facet of neoliberal globalization. The expansion of TECs has come on the heels of de-regulation, privatization, and disempowerment of others.

Neoliberal globalization lies behind the move toward education more broadly as a field of business. In particular in the United Kingdom, education had by the late 1990s turned into a business activity. Pro-market ideologies justified moves to undermine public education authority. According to neoliberal logic, education can be treated as a service like any other. These ideas, espoused by powerful people, worked to turn education into a sector. In fact, international schools in Asia have been created by taking prestigious schools in the United Kingdom and establishing branches elsewhere. Schools like Dulwich and Harrow set up branches in Asia (Bunnell, 2009). Because of such branches, education has been called a UK "export." Wellington College head Anthony Seldon claimed at a conference that "education is one of (the UK's) strongest exports." (*EducationInvestor* March 30, 2009).

Education can be a business that internationalizes without seeming to threaten anyone. Setting up a school overseas is not like moving a factory away; it is more like exporting services. When edu-businesses have a range of schools, they can also tailor services to distinct sections of the global population. These might be luxury private schools but they might also be low-fee for-profit schools in the developing world.

Some of the basic patterns of neoliberalization can be found in education. David Harvey (2005) notes that "accumulation by dispossession" characterizes the way the wealthy expand their resources. The wealthy appropriate public resources, which might serve the collective, and divert them toward their own accumulation. A similar logic can be found in education. In public education, rhetoric of an "education crisis" justifies wresting control away from authorities and giving private actors more influence over schools. As schools are de-regulated in the name of improving education outcomes, private actors swoop in and take over schools. The possibility of this option also encourages collusive ties between public regulators and private interests in schooling, so that the "crisis" of education can be an engineered opportunity and not just good fortune for the companies that gain. A substantial literature points to this logic in education (Saltman, 2000, 2005, 2012; Verger et al., 2016: 119–120).

Attention to the broader forces of neoliberal globalization also helps to situate our subject in history. International school operators have expanded at a particular time in capitalist world development. This period includes several features that facilitate the growth of edu-businesses. First, the neoliberalization of the state in

Europe, by de-regulating education, encouraged the emergence of school operators that could eventually turn their gaze overseas. Second, the de-nationalization of education gives private actors an opportunity to step in. Declining state control over education standards and curricula mean that businesses can gain more influence over education. Third, rising wealth and growing wealth inequality in Asia has created a large market for international school services.

While these wider forces have contributed to the emergence of TECs as international school operators, the pattern of neoliberalization in international schools does not exactly follow what is seen in other fields. For starters, this pattern has grown without the promulgation of an ideology of choice. There are no public debates over the role of markets in international schools. Market creation has not been justified in the name of expanding "school choice." This rhetoric has been common in many contexts where the charter schools or voucher programs were under consideration. The language of choice and "freedom" is also common in broader projects of neoliberalization. Yet that has not been the dominant mode of presenting the shifts in international schools. This story is not one of powerful people latching onto market ideas, nor of weak governments being forced to undertake marketizing reforms. Many of the states where TECs have made inroads in Asia can hardly be called weak. They are certainly not victims of foreign firms. Rather, states have worked actively with these firms. The marketizing effect has thus been more indirect than in many other fields.

Modes of Change in the International School Landscape

The above discussion foregrounds this book's contribution. I introduce four main modes of change involving the business of international schools. Each is a dynamic that points to a surprising or non-intuitive effect.

State Policies Weaken State Regulatory Capacities

The growth of edu-businesses is not an activity that starts and finishes in a market or contained economic sphere. Government policy has been central to the creation and expansion of education firms. Privatization of education, especially in the United Kingdom, has been a crucial driver of growth in education firms. Direct privatization has been a less common policy in Asia. Instead, states in the region have created space for international school commercialization by introducing policies to develop a "knowledge economy" or to make destinations more attractive to foreign business. States designate education hubs with state-supported infrastructure, and they create exceptions to rules on establishing schools or on attendance at schools. Countries in the region—with the sole exception of Malaysia—have refrained from making new laws that directly or in a systematic way allow businesses to operate primary and

8 1 Introduction

secondary schools. The relevant state policies are thus not the same as de-regulation. They usually serve purposes of developing the economy. This purpose has more often meant creating selective market incentives rather than simply preserving markets.

Rather than de-regulation or market preservation, international school policy might be better imagined as a set of government actions that demarcate boundaries of the compulsory school system. International school policies are those that influence the conditions for establishing international schools and who can attend them. These policies are embedded in concerns that stretch beyond international schools.

Thinking of international school policy in terms of demarcating boundaries helps clarify implications of policy changes in recent years. These changes have mostly served to expand the field in which international schools can operate. Doing so simultaneously places fewer protections against markets on the local school system. The local school system can thus be exposed to market forces, posing further dilemmas for states. In this way, states divest themselves of authority over education, even if unwittingly or inadvertently. Thus, even as states in Asia have not pursued de-regulation, a common effect of state policies is that they tend to weaken state regulatory capacities.

International Schools Become Side-Businesses for Other Investments

As TECs have entered international schools, much of the business interest in international schools has become incidental. The financing of international schools tends to occur through investments in other areas spilling over into education. For many firms in the education field, education is only one of their interests. Other interests may be directly or indirectly connection to education more broadly. A few patterns can be seen. Property developers have found that residents would avail themselves of nearby "premium" education opportunities. In China and Malaysia, developers recognized that rather than working with a separate edu-business to establish on-site schools, they could build and operate their own schools within their developments. This path from property development to the international school business is in some ways the simplest: developers have already solved the problems of acquiring land in a place with families. If education is a business, then skills in land acquisition are among the most important for breaking into the sector. In another and possibly overlapping pattern, education is one among a constellation of interests held by a firm. Regardless of the industry in which a firm starts, it can get involved in school-related services. A school's needs for food or trash removal might drive the operator to develop sidelines in catering or waste disposal services.

In another form, the focus is more on investment than in operations. Education has turned into an investment destination. The recession that began in 2008 gave many the lesson that education is relatively unaffected by economic downturns, and that has prompted many asset managers to look to education when building portfolios. Now a number of fund managers maintain education portfolios. Institutional investors turn to these funds, or directly to firms. Consulting related to education has exploded. There are trade publications and conferences, and specialists in the business of education. In addition, fund managers own some of the largest edu-businesses. It is common for the term "education specialist" to be used to describe professionals who focus on the finance of education—but who may no proficiency in pedagogy or traditional schooling matters.

These patterns point to a *financialization* of international education. That is, organizations are oriented increasingly more to their own financial value and less to earning profits from what they produce (educated children). Education itself becomes secondary to maintaining "value." This mode of change also has implications for what happens within schools, as can be seen in pressure on the meanings of "internationalization."

Internationalization Becomes Co-Opted by Corporate Forces

The effort to make education more international stems from a promising motive. Yet what happens in many international schools is that internationalization or globalization becomes a means for corporatization of schooling. This corporatization takes a few forms. First, internationalization can mean supplying a ladder for climbing the global education hierarchy. The purpose of teaching in English, for example, may be to open opportunities to study at "leading" universities in the United States, United Kingdom, Australia, or Canada. Primary and secondary schooling in an international setting is therefore a means to this particular end. "International" may mean little more than that. This point relates to findings in research on international schools that stresses the way parents' class-aspirations shape those schools (Tarc & Tarc, 2014; Wright, Lee, Tang, & Tsui, 2016).

Second, schools can be "international" through their place in a transnational chain of schools. The major operators draw attention to their ownership of schools in many parts of the world. As a result, school officials stress that students join a "global network" of schools. This meaning of international is like a consumer brand. This imaginary also separates students from local contexts (Caffyn, 2010; Wright & Lee, 2014). They are socialized not in any community in the host territory beyond the school's walls, but are tied to students in schools with shared slogans in another part of the world.

Third, "global" citizenship can replace efforts to foster democratic citizenship. International schools stress that students become "global citizens" who are ready for an international environment. While there is certainly good in that mission, it tends to come alongside the abandoning of democratic notions of citizenship. Global citizens are equipped with skills for navigating fluid job markets, and they are linked to famous companies and schools around the world. Students may be exposed to global problems such as climate change. Research on "global citizenship" programs suggests such programs are oriented to preparing students for footloose, corporate careers

(Gardner-McTaggart, 2016). Although values of responsibility may be instilled, these are not tied to a notion of democratic citizenship. This finding fits with the fact that international schools have boomed precisely in illiberal places, such as the Gulf and parts of Southeast Asia.

Through these means, internationalization tends to take a particular, corporate form. In the abstract, "international" or "global" schooling does not need to follow corporate modes of organization. "International" is an understandable aspiration but it is easily appropriated by corporate forces and modes of organization. As shall be seen, even education movements like International Baccalaureate Organisation or United World College, which were founded on non-corporate internationalist principles, have felt pressure to change in this direction. The way schools and parents in Asia treat the IB program, has shifted to become primarily concerned with gaining access to top global universities (Lee & Wright, 2016).

In my capacities working in international schools, I could observe these dynamics first hand. Even a school that had little revenue incentive felt pressure to adopt the "internationalizing" styles of nearby international schools. There is room for non-corporate forms, but such forms are also more difficult. I introduced IGCSE into a school where I worked, with a bilingual twist. This innovation made sense for the particular school. The main pressure, though, is to keep up with other schools. Then, it is not that parents are demanding the best education from the school, but that they want the slogans and brands they hear about other schools having.

Consumer Cultures of Education Deflect Critical Engagement

A framework of meaning has been created around international schools. This framework provides a vocabulary for school officials and parents to discuss education. It helps people, especially parents-cum-consumers, make sense of international schools. Key terms serve as reference points that end discussions rather than prompt further enquiry. An imaginary has been created, with variation from place to place, that allows parents to understand international schools.

These meanings are shared by parents through communities created largely by advertising. Education as a consumer product has become the mode of sharing knowledge and evaluation. This mode is distinct from a citizenship or community mode, in which members simply attend the school affiliated with the group to which they belong. International schools become assessed along the lines of commercial purchases: there are a few brands and a limited range of differences in what is offered, while price becomes a major signal of distinction. This dynamic internalizes the creation of education markets. The effect is powerful: education becomes a family decision in a marketplace. Opportunities for engagement, critique, and questioning are limited. A growing consumer culture in education has been noted in other contexts of compulsory education, such as in public schools in the United States (Saltman, 2000). Reflecting on American public schools, Patricia Burch (2009: 12) writes that "parents become consumers, students become human capital with their education

Modes of Change in the International School Landscape

calculated in rates of return; administrators are expected to act like managers and entrepreneurs." In international schools, where fees have long been high and schools independently-run, this trend has been subtler. It is nonetheless a powerful shift and among the most palpable when meeting parents of international school students or visiting school premises.

The symbolic landscape of international schools offers numerous examples of consumer orientation. The content of school programs, ostensibly close to the core missions of schools, has become a servant of marketing. Schools are said to have "IB teachers"—yet there is no specific training for teachers in IB schools.[1] "Holistic education" presents opportunities for "integrated learning" for students. These might be great pedagogical concepts but they also become marketing slogans. For admissions officers and parents, they are rarely engaged further than as such slogans—the consumer mode does not encourage deeper enquiry. International schools cultivate "global citizenship" but the meaning of a such phrase is seldom elaborated. On top of these buzzwords, other symbols serve branding or cross-branding functions. Schools display their affiliations with world-leading companies, with prestigious universities such as Julliard in music or MIT in engineering, or with world-class athletes as coaches. These affiliations bestow status by association.

There is a contextual, aesthetic aspect to the presentation of international schools. The distinction between the content of education and the way it is marketed recalls theories of art criticism. The philosopher Jacques Derrida (1987), in his comments on art criticism, suggests that the contextual framing of a painting is essential for evaluating it. In making this point, Derrida departs from the Kantian viewpoint that art should be assessed solely on its own merit. He formulates a notion of *parergon*, in which art is viewed against a certain context. International schools are now often marketed in a similar way. Education philosophy and the content of the curriculum are not the main features of how schools are judged, or seek to be judged. Rather, the wider context—facilities, campus size, and global network—has become more important.

Scope and Approach

This book offers a first overview of international school providers. The central concern is specifically with the expansion of these firms. Several related topics thus lie beyond the scope of this study. Since the concern is not primarily with the educational results of these schools, there is little here on student performance. I address curricular and pedagogical matters only insofar as they relate to the organizational changes of schools. The lens here is trained specifically on school operators and

---

[1] For a school to gain IB certification, teachers undergo only the lightest of training programs. As a school administrator, I have known teachers who are disappointed that a school's IB accreditation does not give them an opportunity for further training. I have also observed a teacher transfer from a non-IB school to an IB school without receiving additional training. Nonetheless, many schools allow parents to believe that their teachers have received special IB training.

their schools, with other actors treated in less depth. Teachers and parents, auxiliary service providers, and investors are among the actors who appear in this story but much more might be said about them than is presented here. Furthermore, the book touches on several topics that could, in future, be addressed in much greater depth.

I draw on fieldwork conducted in several countries in the region, including in Malaysia, Indonesia, Singapore, South Korea, and China, as well as in Denmark, Sweden, and the United Arab Emirates. In those places, I met with school administrators, teachers, and parents. These discussions were essential for providing information and perspectives, as well as for suggesting possibilities that I could pursue through further documentary research.

The regional focus in this book is on East and Southeast Asia. In truth, though, any study of international school operators is necessarily global, since schools in one place are likely to be tied to those in another and run by a firm based elsewhere. I have limited the study to edu-businesses holding schools in Asia. The reason for this choice is that the expansion of corporate-run international schools has been most dramatic in this region. These schools are clearly a phenomenon in other parts of the world, as well. A new Nord Anglia school near Dublin recently featured on the board of the Irish version of the classic game Monopoly. It is in Asia, though, that growth has been quickest in recent years. The story spills well beyond Asia. The owners and main investors in the largest school groups in the region are based in the United Kingdom and the Gulf states, as well as in Asia. The focus here is also mostly, though not exclusively, on schools in cities. As a geographically-sensitive literature on international schools notes, these schools can be informed by dynamics at local, national, and global scales (Marginson & Rhoades, 2002; Ledger, Vidovich, & O'Donoghue, 2014).

This subject is not only one that transcends national boundaries; it also forces the researcher to think beyond disciplinary divides. These connections across space and fields are precisely what need highlighting. Links across countries and between government and private actors provide the bases for developments in international schools (Adick, 2018). If edu-businesses were studied from only the perspective of economics, then it would naturalize and de-politicize the creation of an international school *sector*. The sociology of education provides an important anchor for this study, but a wide perspective is needed. Insights from political economy help for capturing the policies that contribute to the creation of markets. We need attention to the shifting perceptions of opportunities by families in Asia. Finally, we need a sensitivity to the values and expectations of parents. Only in combining these approaches can we develop a critical perspective on these new configurations in education.

References

Adick, C. (2018). Transnational education in schools, universities, and beyond: Definitions and research areas. *Transnational Social Review, 8*(2), 124–138.

Au, W., & Hollar, J. (2016). Opting out of the education reform industry. *Monthly Review, 67*(10), 29–37.

References

Ball, S. J. (2009). Privatising education, privatising education policy, privatising educational research: Network governance and the 'competition state'. *Journal of Education Policy, 24*(1), 83–99.

Ball, S. J. (2012). *Global education inc.: New policy networks and the neo-liberal imaginary*. New York: Routledge.

Bunnell, T. (2007). The international education industry. *Journal of Research in International Education, 6,* 349–367.

Bunnell, T. (2009). The exporting and franchising of elite English private schools: The emerging 'second wave'. *Asia Pacific Journal of Education, 28*(4), 383–393.

Burch, P. (2009). *Hidden markets: The new education privatization*. London: Routledge.

Caffyn, R. (2010). 'We are in Transylvania, and Transylvania is not England': Location as a significant factor in international school micropolitics. *Educational Management Administration & Leadership, 38*(3), 321–340.

Chew, P. G.-L. (2009). In pursuit of linguistic gold: Mothering in a globalised world. *English Today, 25*(2), 33–39.

Derrida, J. (1987). *The truth in painting*. Chicago: University of Chicago Press.

Entrich, S. R. (2018). *Shadow education and social inequalities in Japan: Evolving patterns and conceptual implications*. New York: Springer.

Exley, S., Braun, A., & Ball, S. (2011). Global education policy: Networks and flows. *Critical Studies in Education, 52*(3), 213–218.

Gardner-McTaggart, A. (2016). International elite, or global citizens? Equity, distinction and power: The International Baccalaureate and the rise of the South. *Globalisation, Societies and Education, 14*(1), 1–29.

Gardner-McTaggart, A. (2018). The promise of advantage: Englishness in IB international schools. *Perspectives: Policy and Practice in Higher Education, 22*(4), 109–114.

Gulson, K. N., & Lubienski, C. (2014). The new political economy of education policy: Cultural politics, mobility and the market: A response to M. Peters' 'Four contexts for philosophy of education and its relation to education policy.' *Knowledge Cultures, 2*(2), 70–79.

Harvey, D. (2005). *A brief history of Nnoliberalism*. New York: Oxford University Press.

Hayden, M., Levy, J., & Thompson, J. J. (Eds.). (2015). *The SAGE handbook of research in international education* (2nd ed.). Singapore: Sage.

Independent Education Today. (2016, June 27.) Huge global demand for English-medium K-12 Education. Available online at https://ie-today.co.uk/Article/huge-global-demand-for-english-medium-k-12-education/. Accessed May 24, 2019.

Kim, Y. (2016). *Shadow education and the curriculum and culture of schooling in South Korea*. New York: Palgrave Macmillan.

Komljenovic, J., & Robertson, S. L. (2017). Making global education markets and trade. *Globalisation, Societies and Education, 15*(3), 289–295.

Kovacs, P. E. (Ed.). (2011). *The gates foundation and the future of US 'public' education*. New York: Routledge.

Lai, A., & Maclean, R. (2011). Managing human capital in world cities: the development of Hong Kong into an education hub. *Asia Pacific Journal of Education, 31*(3), 249–262.

Lee, M., & Wright, E. (2016). Moving from elite international schools to the world's elite universities. *International Journal of Comparative Education and Development, 18*(2), 120–136.

Ledger, S., Vidovich, L., & O'Donoghue, T. (2014). *Global to local curriculum policy processes: The enactment of the International Baccalaureate in remote international schools*.

Lewis, N. (2011). Political projects and micro-practices of globalising education: Building an international education industry in New Zealand. *Globalisation, Societies and Education, 9*(2), 225–246.

Lubienski, C. (2005). Public schools in marketized environments: Shifting incentives and unintended consequences of competition-based educational reforms. *American Journal of Education, 111*(4), 464–486.

Lui, T.-L. (2014). Opportunities and tensions in the process of educational globalisation: The case of Hong Kong. *Asia Pacific Viewpoint, 55*(2), 132–143.

Marginson, S., & Rhoades, G. (2002). Beyond national states, markets, and systems of higher education: A glonacal agency heuristic. *Higher Education, 43*(3), 281–309.

Molnar, A. (2006). The commercial transformation of public education. *Journal of Education Policy, 21*(5), 621–640.

Olds, K. (2007). Global assemblage: Singapore, foreign universities, and the construction of a 'global education hub'. *World Development, 35*(6), 959–975.

Olds, K., & Robertson, S. L. (2008, April 16). Education cities, knowledge villages, schoolhouses, education hubs, and hotspots: Emerging metaphors for global higher ed. *Global Higher Ed*. Available online at https://globalhighered.wordpress.com/2008/04/16/metaphors/. Accessed May 24, 2019.

Olmedo, A. (2014). From England with love... ARK, heterarchies and global 'philanthropic governance'. *Journal of Education Policy, 29*(5), 575–597.

Roesgaard, M. H. (2006). *Japanese education and the cram school business: Functions, challenges and perspectives of the juku*. Copenhagen: NIAS Press.

Saltman, K. (2000). *Collateral damage: Corporatizing public schools, a threat to democracy*. Lanham, MD: Rowman & Littlefield.

Saltman, K. (2005). *The Edison schools: Corporate schooling and the assault on public education*. New York: Routledge.

Saltman, K. (2012). *The failure of corporate school reform*. Boulder, CO: Paradigm.

Sidhu, G., & Kaur, S. (2011). Enhancing global competence in higher education: Malaysia strategic initiatives. *Journal of Higher Education in the Asia-Pacific, 36*(4), 219–236.

Sidhu, R. (2002). Educational brokers in global education markets. *Journal of Studies in International Education, 6*(1), 16–43.

Tarc, P., & Tarc, A. P. (2014). Elite international schools in the global South: Transnational space, class relationalities and the 'middling' international schoolteacher. *British Journal of Sociology of Education, 36*(1), 34–52.

Verger, A., Lubienski, C., & Steiner-Khamsi, G. (2016). The emergence and structuring of the global education industry: Towards an analytical framework. In A. Verger, C. Lubienski, & G. Steiner-Khamsi (Eds.), *World yearbook of education 2016: The global education industry* (pp. 1–26). New York: Routledge.

Verger, A., Lubienski, C., & Steiner-Khamsi, G. (2017). The emerging global education industry: Analysing market-making in education through market sociology. *Globalisation, Societies and Education, 15*(3), 325–340.

Wright, E., & Lee, M. (2014). Elite international baccalaureate diploma programme schools and inter-cultural understanding in China. *British Journal of Educational Studies, 62*(2), 149.

Wright, E., Lee, M., Tang, H., & Tsui, G. C. P. (2016). Why offer the international baccalaureate middle years programme? A comparison between schools in Asia-Pacific and other regions. *Journal of Research in International Education, 15*(1), 3–17.

Chapter 2
The Creation of an International Education Sector

"When you walk in the entrance and toward the reception desk in any of our schools, you will see an identical pattern welcoming you," a marketing manager at an international school in Dubai tells me as we tour the facilities. Even flowers are arranged the same way at the opening gates as at other schools run by the same firm. Reception desks have the same shapes and angles. You see the logos with the same colors greeting you. In different countries and at different price levels, I visited several international schools under this firm. No matter where in the world I was visiting, it was clear that the school was a part of the company. The visual cues create a sense of familiarity.

"Students all have their own Apple i-Pads," an administrator at another of the company's schools says. Each classroom has a big screen and a Samsung smart board. Kindergarten classrooms are no exception. She tells me that "we work with good companies for good education. Our students from the age of five can make their own e-portfolio." The other facilities follow this pattern. "We have an Olympic-size swimming pool and our coach has trained the national team," her emphasis on facilities continued. A planetarium is on the premises. Students can also enjoy lunch and snacks that are cooked by famous hotel chefs. "Our chef also sends his own kids to our school. That is the best guarantee that the food is good." The argument may be convincing to parents, who may feel as though they are touring a hotel rather than a school.

These striking facilities have become emblematic of international schools. Once a set of community institutions relevant only to a tiny minority, international schools have transformed. They are now economic entities that exist in an international school *sector*—a development less than 15 years old. Schools now compete for students in order to gain revenue, and this competition alters what the schools are and how they approach their work. The proliferation of over-the-top facilities gives expression to this competition. They have internationalized in a way that also implies de-nationalization. International schools are also increasingly tied into transnational

---

© The Author(s), under exclusive license to Springer Nature Singapore Pte Ltd., part of Springer Nature 2019
H. Kim, *How Global Capital is Remaking International Education*, SpringerBriefs in Education, https://doi.org/10.1007/978-981-32-9672-5_2

education corporations (TECs) with interests in multiple countries.[1] Before explaining in later chapters how this transformation has unfolded, in this chapter I document what has changed in international schools.

Traditional International Schools

In the past, international schools catered mostly to the needs of expatriate children and offered education programs resembling those in the "home" society. In colonies, families from the colonizing country relied on international schools to educate their children. Parents, missionaries, or other community members were often the founders of these schools. The schools were clearly separated from the main education system of the country they were located, therefore, and offered programs distinct from the local curriculum. They self-identified as "home country" schools. Students were to gain skills in their national language and have education experiences proximate to what their counterparts at "home" received. Perpetuating a national identity was a core part of international school missions.

Another type of school that might be called an international school served a wider population. A set of colonial schools sought to civilize or enlighten indigenous populations with Western or religious education. For example, in Indonesia, before independence, the Dutch government established Western-style schools in order to educate the local population. There were three different types of schools: for the Dutch, European schools that met standards at home; Chinese schools for ethnic Chinese; and native schools for other locals. The language of education in all of these types of schools was Dutch. Chinese and "native" schools provided Chinese and Indonesian language lessons as well. Highly talented native students or upper-class children could shift into Western secondary education institutions and mix with the colonizers' children (Emerson, 1946: 503).

Another predecessor to today's international schools was the missionary school. In many parts of Asia, missionaries opened schools for the local population. These could offer schooling in either a local or foreign language. In Korea, for example, missionary schools run by Americans and others expanded in the late nineteenth century, and then again after the country's independence from Japan in 1945. In the name of enlightenment, these schools taught Christianity and English. Opportunistic Korean families sent their children to these schools—often without much interest in the religious component—in order to raise their life prospects. It was at these institutions that families could gain exposure to the outside world. Missionary schools cultivated young people who could deliver the Christian message to locals and who became bridges between outside powers and locals. The discipline in these schools

---

[1] I use the term transnational edu-business to refer to revenue-oriented groups that own self-labelled international schools at the K-12 education in multiple countries. My discussion also makes reference to organizations that are formally not-for-profit, since that legal status does not preclude revenue-orientation and global ambition.

also moulded useful workers. A legacy of missionary schools was the creation of a long-lasting network of international Christian schools. A group, the Network of International Christian Schools, set up International Community Schools (ICS), starting from Korea, in 15 countries across Asia, Africa, and South America. These schools follow an American curriculum with Christian mission.

Over the second half of the twentieth century, international schools persisted beyond colonial rule. The colonial purpose disappeared. The schools mainly came to serve the expatriate families of diplomats and private sector representatives. They continued to be separate from local school systems. Many of the students were from families that moved regularly as the breadwinner was posted to different locations. International schools, tied to nations or other missions, served this often-temporary expatriate population. They also served the needs of "third culture kids," those whose cultural identity does not match with their citizenship (Useem & Downie, 1976).

The Creation of an International Education Sector

From serving a very small population, international schools have grown tremendously. The scale of international education has exploded in recent years. ISC Research, a consulting company in the education field that provides numbers on international schools, defines an international school as a school that provides an international curriculum in English, such as British schools abroad, American schools abroad, schools with International Baccalaureate (IB) or International General Certificate of Secondary Education (IGCSE) programs, and sister schools of independent school brands (from, for example, the United Kingdom). At present, there are 9318 international schools world-wide. These schools embrace 5.07 million students from kindergarten to grade 12 (Keeling, 2018). Twenty years ago, there were only some 1000 international schools operating in English (Wechsler, 2017).

Alongside and facilitating this growth in international education has been the emergence of international schools as a sector of economic activity. Here I note four dimensions to this transformation. First, schools compete against each other for students, which can be seen in the emphasis on facilities. Second, schools have stressed a "global" identity as a way of marketing. Third, schools have sought to expand their markets by recruiting local students. Fourth, large transnational firms have entered the international school scene.

Competition

Where international schools once provided a service to those who needed it, they now compete against each other for business. Parents compare options for their children and schools orient a good deal of their energy to attracting and retaining students. In the past, international schools overlapped little in terms of the services they provided.

French families wanted a French education for their children for cultural reasons and also so they could return with minimal disruption to France. British families, or Japanese families had similar ideas. Schools offered distinct services to these communities. Now, though, schools serve a larger *market* of families. Most parents seek an English-language education with a diploma that is internationally-recognized. Schools now aim to satisfy this more homogenous interest. There is, as a result, greater overlap in the sorts of education provided by different schools. Competition is, in turn, an effect of this overlap.

School facilities are a physical manifestation of this competition as I mentioned in the beginning. International schools—almost without exception—give pride of place in their promotion efforts to highlighting their facilities. Tours for prospective parents make swimming pools, auditoriums, and cafeterias focal points for their sales pitches. An effect has been a ratcheting up of spending on facilities. When Cognita and GEMS Education opened new schools in Singapore, each stressed the enormous amount of money spent on facilities. Schools feature Olympic-size swimming pools, planetariums, and chefs from Michelin-starred restaurants. Is a first-grader going to benefit greatly from such facilities? It is hard to see how, but that is beside the point. The norm has become for schools to express their worth in terms of facilities. These may convey a sense that the school has value—and also that a child's attendance there justifies the astronomical fees. The point here is not just that these elite schools have more money to spend on better facilities, but that they invest in facilities as a marketing technique in the context of competition for clients. Schools face pressure to reach out to parents in a way they did not in the past. Parents, for their part, devote more time to discussing the merits of this school or that. Education becomes a product that is consumed.

Building "Global" Identities

Another feature of the marketing efforts of schools is to present themselves as offering a "global" or "international" experience. Promotional material is peppered with the language of "global citizenship." These appeals are backed up with international curricula such as IB and IGCSE; such affiliation indicates to parents that a school has a global orientation. Studying in an IB or IGCSE school may allow their children to have better opportunities to pursue tertiary education in a part of the world of their choosing.

Schools with an international focus have grown in relation to community schools, while international rather than specific foreign programs have encroached on community schools. Many national schools have shifted their names in order to make an international appeal, especially by inserting the word "international" into their name. An Australian School, for example, might change to an "Australian International School." Such shifts reflect that the foreign curriculum is offered alongside another program that is not specific to the country indicated in the name.

The move to "global" education has meant a subtle shift in what international education means. While the term previously indicated a range of non-local school systems, possibly connected to distinct nations, international education increasingly means "not national" or "supranational." The language of "global" seems to capture this denationalization of "international." While international schools once followed distinct foreign curricula, or were inspired by religious tenets, they have now shifted to a more uniform formula (Gardner-McTaggart, 2016).

This development stands in contrast to claims that markets urge providers to differentiate themselves. Parents now may have more choices, but the value of those choices is suspicious. Previously, the international education landscape was more varied, and families sent their children to the school that fit their identity and/or circumstances. The rise of "choice" has necessarily come with the narrowing of this landscape. The choice is between schools that distinguish themselves in terms of facilities or price (Lubienski, 2005: 480–482). Choice is only possible because a large market has been created and replaced a set of communities that once had needs.

The shift to a global orientation may be laudable, both for individual students and for societies more broadly. Taking IB degrees can give students options of studying in many parts of the world, because of the portability of the degrees. Grooming young people with cosmopolitan perspectives can also be good for the future. Yet this shift has brought a particular meaning of "global." This version of global as "not national" has been not so much a celebration of the world's diversity, but a flattening of cultural differences. Schools have become more similar. This globalism is a corporate one, because it is based on the creation of a large market.

Growing the Market: Recruiting Local Students

A component of the creation of a unified international education market is the recruitment of local students into international schools. This shift follows almost logically from others. If international education is no longer focused on providing particular foreign education, but rather on offering a "global" program of value to anyone, then surely it is no longer the exclusive domain of foreign nationals. While restrictions on who can attend international schools vary across Asia, there has been an overall trend of international schools admitting more local students. According to one source, some 80% of students in international schools come from the host countries (Wechsler, 2017). If that figure is taken it seriously, it means that international schools no longer mostly serve expatriate groups.

In some countries, there are clear restrictions forbidding nationals from attending international schools. Yet even in these places, authorities face pressure to "open" international schools to locals. In South Korea, for example, strict laws prohibited Korean nationals from sending their children to international schools, which cater to foreign residents such as American soldiers, missionaries, and the children of diplomats and foreign employees of enterprises. Unable to send their children to these schools, some affluent Korean parents send their children abroad for education. In response, the law was adjusted. As complex legal divisions among foreign education institutions were introduced, Koreans have found ways to enter international schools at home. As discussed in Chap. 4, managing the dividing line between local students and international schools has become central to international education policy.

This point raises questions about the impact of international education on stratification. If international schools are crucial to maintaining a global elite, then this opening may allow groups from other parts of the world to penetrate that elite. On the other hand, to the extent that locals enter international schools, we may see new forms of stratification emerging along class and cultural lines. The wealthy may have access to schools outside the mainstream education system, which could diminish the value of the education system for social mobility. Further, those who experience international education may shift culturally to be more attuned to a cosmopolitan rather than national identity. Both trends might create fractures.

Entrance of School Corporations

The above transformations can all occur without individual schools turning into revenue-oriented enterprises. All schools face the same pressure, so this shift at the school level can be observed. On top of this, though, is the entry of education businesses that manage multiple schools, often in multiple countries. The flattening of the international school landscape suits these firms well. As differences between schools diminish, opportunities for firms emerge. Even as curricula vary, the tasks of operating and promoting schools converge.

> **The Netherlands Inter-community School, Jakarta: From Communal to "Global"**
>
> The Netherlands Inter-community School (NIS) in Jakarta, Indonesia, was established for the purpose of teaching Dutch children. In 1967, it was formalized as a school. For development and expansion, the school received subsidies from the Dutch government. Today, Nord Anglia, one of the biggest TECs, owns NIS. The school's website announces this connection: "NIS: A Nord Anglia Education School." The homepage features a world map with the locations of each Nord Anglia school noted; the page elaborates on the benefits of Nord Anglia ownership: "Our Global Campus: The Global Campus extends learning beyond the classroom through unique challenges and activities. It connects our students around the world to learn together every day, broadening their knowledge and nurturing transferable skills to support their success in school and later in life" (Nord Anglia Education School Jakarta Website). The website of every Nord Anglia international school contains this same image and statement.

The Creation of an International Education Sector 21

Some of the international school operators have become very large. Three of the biggest in Asia are GEMS Education, Cognita, and Nord Anglia. Dubai-based GEMS educates 142,000 students around the world. Cognita's international schools alone have 30,000; Nord Anglia's 20,000. Each of these three firms has annual revenues in recent years between USD 300 million and 500 million (Kim, 2016). The global international school industry is a multi-billion dollar industry, and the largest firms have a global presence. GEMS builds new schools and operates them. Cognita and Nord Anglia have established international schools in Singapore and Hong Kong, respectively, but mostly they acquire existing schools.

The emergence of these TECs means the creation of a whole financial sector around international education. As international school groups have become a target of investment, financial advisory services have mushroomed in this area. Fund managers back international school groups. Consulting firms offer advice to prospective investors. To these actors, international education is purely an economic activity that can be discussed and analysed just like any other sector. News on international schools is as likely to concern their finances as it is to deal with educational matters.

Malaysia's Garden School: A Portrait of Change

Malaysia is home to international schools with histories dating to the British colonial period. The Garden International School is one such school. In 1951, two British women established the Garden School for British children in Malaya. The private school served a clear need at the time. The school continued over the years and was eventually acquired by Taylor's Education Group, one of the biggest private education companies in Malaysia. The group grew through hosting "twinning" programs in tertiary education; in these programs, students attend a local university but gain both local and foreign degrees. Now the group's activities include acquiring and establishing international schools in Malaysia and neighbouring countries. Taylor's renamed the school the Garden International School and repackaged it. It boasts fancier facilities and admits local students as well. It gained recognition as an Apple Distinguished School for guaranteeing that students, teachers, and administrators are provided with Apple devices, which are also used in the classroom.

The construction of an international school sector can be illustrated by describing the international school scene in a particular place. In the next section, I use the example of Singapore for this purpose.

The Shifting International Education Landscape in Singapore

Singapore, with its colonial history and expatriate population, has long had international schools. In 1990, 11 international schools operated in Singapore. But in 2003, the number increased to 23 including local schools that provide foreign education systems (Mok & Yu, 2014). The majority served citizens of specific countries. Others followed particular missions. United World College Southeast Asia (UWCSEA), for example, is part of the worldwide network of 17 UWC schools set up to promote mutual understanding, with the stated aim to "bring together young people from different nations to act as champions of peace" (UWC website). The International School of Singapore (ISS) is a religious school with an American curriculum.

The middle of the first decade of the twenty-first century was a turning point in Singapore's international school sector. The for-profit education chains arrived in 2006. No for-profit chain had an international school in Singapore before that year. In 2007 alone, for example, the Canadian International School opened its fourth campus (before moving to a consolidated central campus), the Australian International School prepared to shift to a new campus to accommodate another 800 students, and the 4000-student strong Global Indian International School (GIIS) was establishing a third campus (Davie, 2007). This period was one not just of new schools but also of many of the existing schools expanding rapidly. By 2012, Singapore's international schools had 38,000 students (Chia, 2012).

Today, schools belonging to international chains have become a prominent part of Singapore's international school scene. There are 35 international schools registered on the island. Fifteen TECs run eighteen international schools in Singapore, some with multiple campuses. Five of these are local firms that also hold a school overseas. The remaining ten have their origins in other countries. Foreign education firms have entered Singapore through a mix of starting new schools and acquiring older ones. Three large firms—Cognita, Nord Anglia, and Taylor's Group—entered through acquisition. Ten of the edu-businesses are for-profit enterprises. The other five are formally non-profits. While this distinction is legally important, non-profit organizations can also be oriented to revenue and expansion.

Table 2.1 shows the groups that run at least one school in Singapore and one abroad. Some of these organizations are small, with just one school in Singapore and an affiliated one elsewhere. Others are very large. The biggest organizations include Nord Anglia, Cognita, GEMS Education, Taylor's Group, and Global Schools Foundation. Nord Anglia is now based in Hong Kong. A publicly-listed company since 2013, Nord Anglia holds ten schools in Asia, including five in China under the 'British School' and 'British International School' labels. Cognita, the owner of Singapore's Australian International School as well as its Stamford American International School, has international schools in Vietnam and Thailand. Run by private equity firms since its inception in 2004, Cognita also holds dozens of independent schools in the United Kingdom. GEMS Education claims to be the world's largest chain of schools. GEMS has many schools in the Middle East, India, the UK and the

The Shifting International Education Landscape in Singapore

Table 2.1 Education groups with international schools in Singapore (2016)

Provider	Place founded	Founding year	Year in Singapore	Profit status	School names
United World College	UK	1962	1971	Non-profit	United World College of South East Asia
ISS Education Group	Singapore	1981	1981	For profit	International School Singapore (ISS)
Overseas Education Limited	Singapore	1991	1991	For profit	Overseas Family School (OFS)
Network of International Christian Schools	South Korea (now US)	1983 (reorganized 1992)	1993	Non-profit	International Community School (ICS)
EtonHouse International Education Group	Singapore	1995	2001	For profit	Middleton International School; EtonHouse
Global Schools Foundation	Singapore	2002	2002	Non-profit	Global Indian International School (4 campuses); One World International School (2 campuses)
Delhi Public School Society	India	1949	2004	Non-profit	DPS International School
Huijia Education Group	China	1993	2006	For profit	Hillside World Academy (previously Chinese International School)
Yuvabarathi	India	2005	2007	For profit	Yuvabarathi International School

(continued)

Table 2.1 (continued)

Provider	Place founded	Founding year	Year in Singapore	Profit status	School names
Cognita	UK	2004	2009	For profit	Stamford American International School; Australian International School
Taylor's Education Group	Malaysia	1969 (reorganized 2000)	2011	Non-profit	Nexus International School
Nord Anglia	UK (now Hong Kong)	1972	2012	For profit	Dover Court International School
GEMS Education	UAE	1968 (reorganized 2000)	2014	For profit	GEMS World Academy
Dulwich College International	UK	1619 (reorganized 2003)	2014	For profit	Dulwich College Singapore
White Lodge Education Group	Singapore	1999	2014	For profit	Melbourne Specialist International School

Note This table is a complete list (as of 2016) of organizations that hold at least one international school in Singapore and at least one school overseas. "Year in Singapore" refers to the first year of operating an international school in Singapore, though the group may have earlier operated another educational institution in Singapore. However, OFS now holds just one campus in Singapore, though it is still a publicly-listed company.

United States. Taylor's Group comes from neighboring Malaysia, where it holds a range of private education businesses. Global Schools Foundation, which started the Global Indian International School (GIIS), differs from the above firms because it got its start in Singapore and because it is a nonprofit organization. From its founding in the early 2000s, the group has expanded with the establishment of GIIS-brand schools in a host of Asian countries. In 2015, GIIS acquired One World International School from Garodia, an India-based firm with interests in education and real estate which set up the school in Singapore in 2008.

Traditional international schools now occupy a smaller proportion of the international school landscape. Only seven international schools are single-campus, non-profit schools dedicated to serving a particular community (though they accept expatriates from a variety of backgrounds). The community schools had previously been the mainstay of international education. The ones that remain are mostly older; they were all founded between 1912 and 1999. Some traditional international schools, like

The Shifting International Education Landscape in Singapore 25

the Australian International School and Dover Court International School in 2007 and 2014, were acquired by chains. A related trend that has eaten into the traditional international school scene is the increase in for-profit schools. A few long-standing international schools, such as the Overseas Family School, had operated on a for-profit basis before the 2000s but these were a minority. Now, nearly half of all international schools are formally for-profit. Schools that appear to be affiliated with a community, such as the Canadian International School, are actually local for-profit ventures with no community links. The community schools that remain face competition from for-profit schools with similar names. The American International School was the only "American" school until the transnational firm Cognita established the for-profit Stamford American International School in 2009.[2]

Franchised

At 11 am on a sunny Saturday, I walked into an open house held by an international school. This school is a franchisee of a brand that has rapidly grown to have operations around the region. Two friendly staff members welcomed me and guided me to a gymnasium. Each staff member, including teachers and administrators, had a clear job to do—noting down visitors' information and checking their children's ages. There were between 100 and 150 people in attendance. Coffee, bread, and fruit were on offer in a corner of the gymnasium. A grey-haired principal with a nice smile gave a 20 min presentation. He introduced himself as an educator who has 17 years of experience in the UK and 10 years in international schools. When he started talking about the curriculum, he compared the national education of the UK with the International Baccalaureate, the most popular international education program at present. He said that the UK education system is good, but that the curriculum is focused on tests. With IB, students can be more engaged and less oriented to examinations. IB, therefore, makes possible what cannot be done in the UK system. As with other international schools that I visited, he emphasized the school's position in a global network, its international curriculum, and the facilities. Since the campus is humble compared to other international schools—a half-million Singapore dollars investment in facilities is small in comparison with other schools—he emphasized the friendly atmosphere at the school. He stressed three traits that the school aims to instill in students: that they are 'confident,' are 'capable,' and gain 'global citizenship.' Students would gain a 'holistic' education, a phrase that is often-repeated in education worldwide today. After the speech, staff members conducted tours for parents.

In a short period, this school group expanded from early education to full K-12 international schools. Now over 100 schools in Asia use the label of the firm.

---

[2]Parents are aware that this school is somehow distinct from the first American school. As one mother seeking an international school put it, "SAIS is not a real American school" (an expat mother in Singapore, 2015).

> At each school, students where the same school uniforms with the same logo. The style directly recalls that of traditional British boarding schools, though this firm was founded in Asia. The franchise strategy has been remarkably successful. The school group offers its brand to those interested in operating international schools. The group provides training for operators, who then open schools under the franchise name.

Conclusion

The meaning of "international school" has undergone a profound shift since the early 2000s. Where international schools once catered to the needs of expatriate families from different communities, there is now an international school sector. Private investment in this field has transformed the international school landscape. As nation-specific schools have declined, "international" and "global" have become buzzwords. Schools are keen to attach themselves to symbols that reflect these terms. Adopting IB or IGCSE programs is one manifestation of this trend. Moreover, the creation of this sector has involved the emergence of major transnational corporations that make money from international schools. These investments take a range of forms, including private firms, publicly-listed ones, and those operated by hedge funds. The startling rise of education businesses in the international school "sector"—which they helped create—is a major phenomenon which deserves public attention. In the next chapter, I introduce the origins of these education firms.

References

Chia, S. (2012, April 4). State land for international school's growth to ensure enough 'high-quality places'. *The Straits Times*.

Davie, S. (2007, September 17). Expats hit by space crunch at international schools here: Some deterred from coming here as they face long waiting list for kids to enter school. *The Straits Times*, p. 4.

Emerson, Rupert. (1946). Education in the Netherlands East Indies. *Journal of Negro Education*, 15(3), 494–507.

Gardner-McTaggart, A. (2016). International elite, or global citizens? Equity, distinction and power: The International Baccalaureate and the rise of the South. *Globalisation, Societies and Education*, 14(1), 1–29.

Keeling, A. (2018, February). Investment in international schools: An expanding market. *Educationinvestor Global*, 20–21. https://www.iscresearch.com/uploaded/images/Publicity/EIFeb18_Investment_in_international_schools_an_expanding_market.pdf. Accessed July 11, 2018.

Kim, H. (2016). The rise of transnational education corporations in the Asia-Pacific. *The Asia-Pacific Education Researcher*, 25(2), 279–286.

References

Lubienski, C. (2005). Public schools in marketized environments: Shifting incentives and unintended consequences of competition-based education reforms. *American Journal of Education, 111*(4), 464–486.

Mok, K., & Yu, K. (2014). Introduction—The quest for regional hub status and transnationalization of higher education: Challenges for managing human capital in East Asia. In K. Mok & K. Yu (Eds.), *Internationalization of higher education in East Asia* (pp. 1–26). London and New York: Routledge.

Useem, R. H., & Downie, R. D. (1976). Third-culture kids. *Today's Education, 65*(3), 103–105.

Wechsler, A. (2017, June 5). The international-school surge. *The Atlantic*. https://www.theatlantic.com/education/archive/2017/06/the-international-school-surge/528792/. Accessed April 14, 2018.

Chapter 3
The Origins of International School Groups

The transformation of international education involves activities linking different parts of the planet. Three sets of forces established the basis for transnational education firms. The first, involved in creating these firms, was the promulgation of neoliberal education reforms in the West. Those reforms created private firms specializing in education. For those firms to go abroad required a second factor. This was a global one: that education could be de-nationalized, unhooked from national education systems, as aspirations and infrastructure for education converged globally. This meant that a product could be legible in different places. Third, these firms took off in Asia due to this region's internalization of global education hierarchies and the money available for educational pursuits.

I focus in this chapter on the largest firms. Local firms can become massive among international schools within particular countries. This is especially the case in, for example, Malaysia and China. However, the transnational education firms are mostly ones that got their start outside of the region. For that reason, it is necessary to look beyond the region for their origins.

This chapter tells the global story that set the basis for some of the largest industry players to begin and grow. A starting point here is that we cannot understand the growth of international schools in Asia without thinking about reforms in other corners of the globe. They were interconnected. From another angle, despite all the attention given to neoliberal reforms and their domestic impacts, less attention has been given to the impact in distant places. That is, Britain's reforms in the 1980s and 1990s created firms that are influential across the world. We also need to understand Sweden's education reform as helping to light the fuse that set off the boom in corporatized international education. Before taking these subjects up, we should first place international schools in the context of the "global education industry" (Verger, Lubienski, & Steiner-Khamsi, 2016).

© The Author(s), under exclusive license to Springer Nature Singapore Pte Ltd., part of Springer Nature 2019
H. Kim, *How Global Capital is Remaking International Education*, SpringerBriefs in Education, https://doi.org/10.1007/978-981-32-9672-5_3

International Schools and the Global Education Industry

The past two decades have seen spaces for industry to grow tremendously in education. As these spaces have grown, firms too have expanded to dominate a few of the spaces and to stretch across spaces. In the United States, big firms have emerged around testing services, textbooks, and charter schools (Au & Hollar, 2016; Molnar, 2006). Large edu-business, often with connections to property development, have made their way into elite education and international school provision in places such as Spain (Olmedo, 2013) and the United Arab Emirates (Ridge, Kippels, & Shami, 2016). In lower-income countries, private-public partnerships—advocated for by the World Bank and other international institutions—have increased in education, ostensibly to boost student enrolments and improve education quality (Srivastava & Walford, 2016). More broadly, globalization of standards has created economies of scale that private firms can take advantage of in order to build transnational education markets (Verger, Steiner-Khamsi, & Lubienski, 2017).

The international education business is part of the global education industry. Firms operating international schools are connected to other parts of the global education industry. These connections include through firms that both operate international schools and have interests in other areas of education, such as preschool centers ("early education"). Investors with education portfolios may have holdings in both international school operators and a range of other education firms. Consultancies in education investment and management deal with multiple types of education, possibly advising clients on whether to invest more in an international school chain or in a tutoring company. International school providers can also form relationships with private vendors who supply textbooks, school software, or electronics equipment. These are ways that international schools have become tied into the global education industry.

We can consider some examples. If we look at the supply chain for international schools, we can see these linkages. International schools have become increasingly prominent as clients for firms in education supply chains. One supplier of technology services, Finalsite expanded rapidly in the international school sector. The US-based firm, which offers "web solutions for schools," had just one international school as a client in 2007; by 2014 one quarter of the company's business came from this sector (Glass, 2014) and it had offices in Bangkok and London. Another set of services includes student recruitment. Agencies link students aspiring to study in another country to international schools abroad. This service reflects the trend of international schools serving neither expatriates nor local populations but rather students from abroad who may have limited choices in their own country.

We can also find examples of firms active in international education and another education area. The International Primary Curriculum program, a curriculum, is under World Class Learning (WCL) Group, a firm formed in 1998 to set up international schools in the United States. WCL runs a network of international schools in the US, Europe, and the Arabian Gulf. In 2013, WCL merged with Nord Anglia.

Firms like Nord Anglia are thus not just operators of schools but are closely tied to other aspects of the education economy.

Other services are targeted more toward the business end of international schools. A set of consultancies has emerged that provide advice on how to manage international schools. The International Schools Consultancy (ISC) produces research reports on the "industry." UK-based Prospects Group offers advice on management and curriculum development; its subsidiary, Gabbitas, specializes in student recruitment. Prospects helps UK schools pass Office for Standards in Education (Ofsted) inspections. Its website states that its "consultants all have extensive knowledge of the Ofsted inspection framework" (Prospects). In other words, many have worked for Ofsted. Not only does the firm advise schools on passing Ofsted inspections, it also carries out inspections on behalf of Oftsed. The lines between independent and official interests is particularly blurred in the UK's education system. Such services generate income: in 2013–14 Prospects earned GBP 80 million in revenue. Further services for investors included trade magazines, such as *Education Investor*, which provides monthly updates on all aspects of for-profit education. The profession of education consultant did not exist in the mid-2000s. Now it is a thriving field that includes specialists in international schools. Expertise in education now means knowledge of education as a business.

We see now that international education, as a business, is implicated in a larger global education industry. The incorporation of international schools into this industry has occurred quickly. At the turn of the century, most international schools were islands, operating independently for a community. While some schools have resisted corporatization, that has not prevented international education from becoming a business.

Education Reforms and the Rise of Education Firms

Policies implemented in the name of making markets freer and giving individuals more choice have been attempted in a wide range of areas of life. Milton Friedman is the figure most often associated with the neoliberal orthodoxy that de-regulation and privatization can best serve public interests. Friedman argued that his ideas be applied to education, just as to other spheres. For a long period, though, education remained the responsibility of public authorities. While other activities saw government roles diminish, education remained something provided by the state. In parts of the Western world in the 1990s, though, states began to apply neoliberal thinking to education. This move had significant consequences.

The effects of neoliberal policies in spheres other than education serve as a guide to what might be expected in education. Big, well-connected firms tend to gain advantages. In Pinochet's Chile, where Friedman's Chicago Boys seized an opportunity to implement their ideas, powerful American firms were well-placed to gain from the openings of privatization and de-regulation. Rather than competitive markets, oligopolies emerged in some sectors. With unions quieted, workers had few representatives in politics. Instead of everyone gaining, inequality widened (Klein, 2008, Chap. 3).

In education, too, parallel policies can be expected to foster firms that use connections and size to grow even bigger. There is an extensive literature on the consequences of "school choice" reforms. Much research on education privatization and corporatization addresses the rise of for-profit school operators. Here my focus is on how reforms created, or enlarged, firms that would later go overseas and invest in international education.

Sweden: Lighting the Fuse

The story of reforms begins in an unlikely place: social democratic Sweden. In education, as in other fields, Sweden has an established record of prioritizing fairness and public provision over "choice" and private options. By the late 1980s, Sweden had not embraced neoliberal principles to the extent that the United Kingdom and the United States had. In education, too, the two Anglophone countries introduced pro-business measures before Sweden. Still, in the early 1990s, Sweden introduced a radical, market-creating education policy. The effects of this policy are worth considering here for two purposes: first, for their role in creating education firms that would later run elite international schools overseas; and, second, for inspiring and helping to legitimize pro-business reforms in education elsewhere, particularly in Britain.

The Swedish government launched its free school policy in 1992. In the context of a social democracy, the most business-friendly education policies were suddenly put in place. Private education providers were permitted to own schools. The government offered vouchers to pay school operators. Parents could exercise choice, in theory, over which school they would like their children to attend. The Swedish government went further than simply allowing private entities to operate schools. The free school policy even allowed private providers to obtain profit from school operations. And the Swedish government funded these schools, subsidizing 100% of each student's fee (Wiborg, 2015: 475–476). The policy was intended to encourage small groups of parents to set up schools in their communities. Public discussions suggested that the free school policy would give rise to independent schools, each oriented to the needs and values of local communities. While independent schools have not come to dominate the education system, they remain significant. In 2010, more than ten percent of compulsory education students were in independent schools (Sahlgreen, 2010).

An unintended consequence of the free school policy was the rise of education firms that grew into chains. As chains, they could out-compete independent schools. In 1993, a private education firm, Internationella Engelska Skolan (IES) started. Another private education firm, Kunskapsskolan, was founded in 1999 and opened a new school the following year. As these firms grew, they sought partners as sources of finance. IES partnered with an American firm in order to fund expansion. In some instances, the ordering has been reversed. Private equity firms jumped into the business of launching schools. With guaranteed government money, running schools was a safe and potentially lucrative place for savings. Both of the above-named firms have since expanded their operations domestically and internationally.

The example set by these companies was seized by "school choice" reformers overseas, most notably in Britain. Education Secretary Michael Gove rushed to herald Sweden's free school policy. Having support from the British government, Kunskapsskolan established Learning Schools Trust in 2010 in the UK as a charitable organization through which the for-profit firm could operate schools that had been given low evaluations. Kunskapsskolan now operates one international school in India and one in Saudi Arabia. It is not one of the top international school operators in Asia, but its history demonstrates the linkage between today's international schools in Asia and earlier education policy change outside of Asia.

Faced with a small set of large firms running schools and receiving criticism, the Swedish government has begun to turn away from the free school policy. JB Education, one of the for-profit education firms, abruptly closed down free schools and students lost their seats suddenly. Social segregation has also worsened since the early 1990s (Wiborg, 2014). Sweden received a warning in a report published in 2015 by the OECD, asserting that "Sweden's school system is in need of urgent change" (Wigmore, 2016). There is little evidence that the free school reform improved quality of education for many. More recently, Education Minister Gustav Fridolin declared that the free school policy was a "political failure" (Weale, 2015).

The United Kingdom: Private Education Businesses Take off

The year 1992 also marked a major moment in British education policy. The Office for Standards in Education (Ofsted) was established that year and began to conduct regular inspections of all schools. Previously, inspections were organized locally; under the new policy, a centralized body would undertake inspections of all schools. To address the problem of poorly performing schools, private operators were permitted to enter and help improve school management. This measure gave firms a role to play in running schools (Earley, 1998).

By the early 2000s, UK education policy had set the basis for the emergence of international education firms. Tony Blair praised the Swedish free school policy in a 2005 white paper. Five years later, Education Secretary Gove, having visited Sweden several times, led the passage of the UK's free school policy. Although free schools are state funded schools, they are independently managed and can receive revenue from different sources. Unlike in Sweden, under this policy school operators should not be for-profit entities. Still, the new policy gave many chances for private education firms to work with the government and operate these schools. Sweden's IES was among the first groups to begin organizing free schools in Britain. Gove pushed to allow for-profit enterprises to run schools, but was unsuccessful in convincing the government. Private entities now can operate schools, which are subject to inspection by Ofsted two years after opening.

Britain, the Pioneer of Private Education

In 1997, Islington Green School in UK received notice that it was a 'failing school.' An inspection by the Office for Standards in Education (Ofsted) in May had drawn this conclusion; the following month, Her Majesty's Inspectors (HMI) agreed. The year 1997 was an important one for British politics. The Labour Party won a general election against the Tory government. The new prime minister, Tony Blair, came from Islington Green. The school must have been proud to have their graduate at No. 10 Downing Street, even if Blair had opted not to send his children to the school. Islington Green School was not the very top school but it had a good reputation, especially for a school with children from a mix of class backgrounds. GCSE results were even on the upswing. The result from Ofsted and HMI that the school was 'failing' was thus a shock to teachers, parents, and students.

The 1997 decision sent the school into a downward spiral. Performance declined. Many teachers left. Violent incidents involving students occurred. Parents took their children out of the school; some students, feeling responsible for the school's performance, even volunteered to leave. GCSE results put the school in the bottom two percent of all schools nationally (Smithers, 2005). While teachers and parents abandoned the school, one teacher, Ken Muller, remained committed. Muller refused to accept the evaluation results. Under the Freedom of Information Act, he applied for Ofsted and HMI documents 11 years after the dreadful evaluations of 1997 (Ibid.). He found that the HMI team had unanimously concluded that the school was fine. However, then Chief Inspector Chris Woodhead chose to overlook the HMI recommendation and followed the decision of Ofsted instead. At that time, Woodhead classified 265 schools as requiring "special measures" (Wallace, 2005). Islington Green School was one of them.

In 2002, a so-called progressive and young headteacher, Trevor Averre-Beeson, joined the school. Tony Blair's former speech writer, Peter Hyman, also started a new career as a teacher at Islington Green in 2004. That same year, Absolute Return for Kids (ARK), a non profit organization, announced that they would operate the school (Ibid.). The local community, led by teachers, protested against ARK's intervention; after continued protests, ARK decided to withdraw the plan. After the episode, Averre-Beeson left the school and became the founder of Lilac Sky Schools, one of the UK's biggest for-profit education firms. The business later changed its name to Lilac Sky Schools Academy Trust. Running a chain of schools, the firm proposed to transform poorly performing state schools into for-profit schools. Ironically, Lilac Sky Schools Academy Trust was forced to close and in 2017 investigation into alleged financial impropriety and mismanagement began (BBC News, 2017; Dickens, 2017). Hyman, meanwhile, went on to become the principal of School 21, a free school.

International Schools and the Global Education Industry 35

> There are various theories to explain why the education authorities failed Islington. Politics offers a possible reason. Labour needed to show it could make tough decisions (Johnson, 2012). Islington Green became a scapegoat, Muller argued. Islington's failure was part of the Blair administration's 'naming and shame policy.' The government was unafraid to show it would punish even a school attended by the prime minister. Another theory is that the move was a deliberate effort to privatize education. Chief Inspéctor Woodhead, who stepped down from that post in 2000, went on to found edu-business Cognita in 2004. The Ofsted inspector who failed Islington, Elizabeth Passmore, later joined GEMS. Mike Tomlinson, who was then director of inspection, followed Passmore to GEMS (Wallace, 2005). Those who marked Islington as a struggling school later built careers running for-profit schools.

This sudden change of policy contributed to the birth of large private education companies for schools from early education through secondary education in the UK and international schools in other countries. Both Cognita and Nord Anglia have expanded with the neolibral turn in education policy in the UK since the 1990s. Cognita got its start in 2004 when it was founded by Chris Woodhead and a private equity firm. Woodhead, a former teacher and education lecturer, had served as chief inspector at the Office for Standards in Education (Ofsted) from 1994 to 2000. Experience in that role surely helped Woodhead gain a sense for which schools Cognita should acquire. The firm's foundation was laid through acquisition of UK schools; only later did it start buying schools abroad. Nord Anglia was founded in 1972 by Kevin McNeany, another former teacher. Initially, the company provided English lessons for non-native speakers. The firm took off in the 1990s with the UK government's move to take education out of the hands of local authorities. Nord Anglia shifted its focus to purchasing primary and secondary schools. McNeany, who is a vocal advocate of privatizing education, expanded Nord Anglia through purchasing schools that the UK government forced to privatize under the pretext of the underperformance. Like Cognita, Nord Anglia expanded overseas after having consolidated the core of its business in the UK.

The privatization of schools in the UK also created a class of "professionals" who have circulated between government and private sector education positions, including in transnational education corporations (TECs) that operate in the Asia Pacific. The shifting of key Ofsted personnel into large international school groups is an example of that. Passmore, the former Ofsted head of school improvement who left for GEMS Education, later returned to government as Chief Schools Adjudicator. Proximity to the instruments of UK school regulation is an asset for those operating global education firms.

While these effects might be described as unintended consequences of neoliberal reforms in Britain, some government efforts are more directly related to supporting British firms in overseas education "markets." The UK government itself has seemed to be actively involved in reshaping education beyond the country's boundaries. In

2013, the government announced that it would support UK school chains as they sought opportunities overseas. This decision encouraged the growth of international schools in other countries. British withdrawal from the European Union has only intensified this trend. Brexit raises obstacles to bringing foreign students into the country. Early evidence indicates that the announcement of Brexit has produced a bump in student numbers in international schools in other parts of Europe (Sims, 2017). British education operators therefore have greater incentives to invest in their overseas operations. British-run international schools overseas substitute for the revenue international students in the UK would have brought in. Evidence of this logic can already be found.

The United States: From Business to Education

As in Britain, the United States initiated school reforms in the 1990s. The rise of educational management organizations (EMOs) in the 1990s opened schools to private management in a variety of education areas. Privatization of supplementary services expanded rapidly, in areas such as food, transportation, vending machines, and building maintenance (Burch, 2009: 4). Management based on cost efficiency became a norm for schools. Private companies could operate schools as charter schools. In the early 2000s, the George W. Bush administration's No Child Left Behind Act (NCLB) further instilled market ideas into school operations. Test score outcomes became the basis for evaluating school performance and allocating public resources. Rather than becoming active participants in their children's education, parents were treated as customers who were provided with feedback. Armed with information on their children's test performances and on teachers' qualifications, parents could make "choices" about their children's education. They could opt to send their children to another school if the performance was unsatisfactory.

Educationist Patricia Burch describes private corporations expanding their businesses from one sub-sector of education to another. She offers the example of a firm that expanded from providing testing services to school assessment, then to curriculum development, and finally to teacher management. Firms such as these became "experts" in the business of multiple aspects of education. Such firms became crucial in the management of charter schools (Burch, 2009: 33–34). A business selling technical services to a school could become a major player influencing education.

US-based firms in a range of education-related areas later expanded globally and, in some cases, into school management. Pearson Education, for example, is best known for its textbooks and assessment services. Alan Singer describes Pearson as a corporate "octopus" for the numerous arms it has in different education-related industries (Singer, 2017). The Pearson Global Schools arm provides supplementary materials to international schools. The firm also runs the Pearson International Schools Community (PISC), a forum where educators and parents can receive updates related to all aspects of international schools (PISC website).

There are more direct linkages between privatization of schools in the United States and international school groups. Two examples are especially prominent and they point to a possibly dubious side of the education business. Michael Milken is a financier and philanthropist who has been involved in the health and education sectors for decades. He established Knowledge Universe, a firm dedicated to operating mostly early childhood centers. Knowledge Universe expanded overseas, acquiring hundreds of nurseries in Southeast Asia. Milken is also a convicted felon (Cohan, 2017). Another convicted criminal and education entrepreneur is Chris Whittle. He spent time in prison in the early 1990s for financial crime. Later, he established one of the largest chains of charter schools, the Edison Schools (Saltman, 2005). The chain eventually collapsed in 2003. Soon after, Whittle began planning to build a brand of elite international schools called Avenues. The extravagant flagship campus is in New York, and branches are to be opened in a number of global cities. Financier-felon-educationists like Milken and Whittle do not operate the most prominent international school groups but they are influential actors in this field.

In the United States, school policies have made businesses on the fringes of education (such as textbooks) or completely outside of education (e.g., finance) enter schools. These organizations do not begin with ideas about pedagogy but with business know-how. Their expertise is in running for-profit companies. Yet they have transformed themselves into educationists, at least in name. Many of these firms have, in turn, sought opportunities across the world. US-based international school providers remain on the margins of Asia's international education scene, but this pattern contributed to the ethos of international education as a global business.

De-nationalization as a Force for Edu-Business Entry into International Education

For firms to operate successfully in diverse contexts, they must be able to offer a service that can be seen as valuable in many different places. Once a standardized product or template is found for offering the service, then firms can take advantage of economies of scale. They can expand and earn more revenue from further expansion. Education does not necessarily lend itself to this approach. Where students are evaluated by teachers, or where curricula are determined by school boards or instructors, education can have a strong local component. Only when an assessment or diploma is made identical across a large population can firms find an advantage. Within national contexts, standardization of assessment can have the effect of creating large markets for supplementary training or textbooks. Firms can then step in.

What has enabled economies of scale in international education? Achieving such economies may be especially difficult on the global scale. After all, across countries, diversity in education needs is only greater. One force has been the rise of technical ways of discussing and assessing education. PISA (Programme for International Student Assessment) scores offer an example. Since PISA examinations are taken around the world, they offer an international standard. The comparative performance of countries can then be assessed. PISA scores create a hierarchy and a public discussion that usually internalizes the notion that higher PISA scores are desirable.

A scheme such as PISA is far from neutral. It removes all discussion of the goals of education, which likely differ from education system to education system. Such differences are replaced with an unquestioning pressure to improve PISA results. This emphasis displaces the purpose of education within a democratic system. A PISA assessment has nothing to do with the goals of education in fostering critical citizens who participate as responsible members of society. Instead, places can be compared according to how well individual students are equipped with measurable skills and knowledge. These skills and knowledge are only one part of what education is for. As schemes like PISA downplay the state's role in defining educational goals, they can be said to represent a de-nationalizing force.

While international schools, located beyond school systems, need not be concerned with PISA results, the discourse of education evaluation encouraged by PISA is relevant. This discourse encourages educationists and parents to think about education in technical terms. Once thinking is done in those terms, then international school groups can compete to claim to offer the best "results."

Another de-nationalizing force is the spread of programs like IB and IGCSE. Such programs disconnect curricula and pedagogy from national education programs. An education ministry is not necessary to run an IB school. Firms could step in where embassies might have been helpful before. Further, a private enterprise can set up schools offering IB diplomas in any part of the world. For transnational edu-businesses, IB makes entering a new territory easier.

Demand in Asia for International Schools

For several linked reasons, transnational education firms have found Asia to hold the biggest opportunities for international school expansion. Middle classes in the region, some newly affluent, have internalized the global education hierarchy as a guide to aspirations. The top-ranked universities in the United States and the United Kingdom have become the places parents wish their children to enroll. Bookshops in Beijing and Seoul sell titles with tips on getting into top universities. Employers in the region also see these overseas degrees as the strongest qualifications. These trends began a few decades ago, with South Korean and Taiwanese becoming among the largest groups of foreign students in US universities. Chinese students subsequently surged in numbers, as parents have sought to secure overseas degrees for their children (Ma & Garcia-Murillo, 2018).

An effect of the value placed on "world-class" universities is to create demand for a secondary school experience that is legible to universities in other parts of the world. If students in Asia are to enter universities abroad, then they need to make themselves attractive to admissions departments. Gaining strong English skills is one component of this task. Attending an English-language secondary school is one of the best ways to gain those skills, though not the only. Beyond language, students need to demonstrate that their education has been a high-quality one. It is here that the de-nationalization of education becomes relevant. Known international schools and diploma programs such as IB or IGCSE are valuable here for demonstrating that a student in Asia may be qualified to pursue a degree at, say, an American university. Many middle-class families in Asia thus aspire to put their children into international schools so that they have better chances of scaling the global education hierarchy (Lee & Wright, 2016).

Middle-class families have also demonstrated a willingness to spend household income on their children's education. This willingness, which has been called "education fever" in South Korea, may have contributed to achieving high rates of education attendance in parts of the region (Seth, 2002). It has also led to massive economies devoted to supplementary education. Especially in the wealthier parts of the region, "cram schools" have become a central feature of the neighborhood landscape. Even as public education is free (or inexpensive) and well-attended in places such as South Korea, Japan, Taiwan, Singapore, and Chinese cities, sending children to supplementary and privately-operated after-school programs has become a norm (Entrich, 2018; Kim, 2016; Roesgaard, 2006). These cram schools teach foreign language, mathematics, or any subject. In most places, they are run as a separate, loosely regulated sector in contrast to strictly regulated public education institutions. Pupils may even attend classes to preview for the next school year's subject matter. When many students do this, then teachers in public schools in effect simply review what most students have already learned. There are, of course, many concerns related to the cram school phenomenon. These range from worries about children's welfare to problems with unqualified teachers to exacerbating inequality.

For our purposes, a key point about supplementary education programs is that families are spending significant portions of their income on their children's education—even in the context of basically free public education. In South Korea, for example, with nearly 70% of students attending cram schools, families spend an estimated USD 1.9 billion annually on shadow education (Kim, 2016: 4–5). Even in the face of global economic recession, middle-class families in Asia continued to spend money on education. In this context, fee-based international schools can appear as an alternative to public schools plus attending cram schools. That is, families may see that income spent on cram schools could go instead to fees for enrolling in an international school, which may claim also to offer a higher quality education and a more "international" one than what the public school system provides. While fees at international schools are high, sometimes astronomical, they should be compared against the large sums that families are already spending on supplementary courses. In this view, the cost of international schools relative to the alternative is not as high as it would be in places where private spending on education is not the norm.

As a result of this calculation and of the desire for "international" qualifications, a pattern that has emerged is for children in the region to migrate to places where they can gain entry into schools that will help them reach global universities. That is, they opt out of national education systems and seek education overseas, including in international schools overseas (Brooks & Waters, 2010; Collins, 2013; Collins, Sidhu, Lewis, & Yeoh, 2014). This trend means that international schools do not necessarily serve local expatriates but actually attract students from abroad. This shift is a profound one in the purpose of international schools. In some cases, whole or partial families move; in others, children are left with legal guardians, found through education agencies, while they pursue their studies. These trends indicate high levels of transnational mobility, among secondary school graduates entering university, among younger students and their families seeking desirable schools abroad, and among edu-businesses seeking to operate schools (Collins, 2013; Falk & Graf, 2016; Mok, 2012). While some of these students leave the region, especially for the UK, many move to other Asian locations. This pattern creates a push into international schools in Asia in two ways. First, the possibility of attracting students from other parts of Asia encourages schools in certain parts of the region to expand. For example, international schools in Malaysia often have students in Korea and in Singapore in mind as a market. Second, countries that lose students to education migration then feel pressure to lure those students back. Education firms offering international schools stand to find opportunities from these trends.

Given that Asian families have internalized the global education hierarchy and have demonstrated a capacity to spend household income to scale it, international school operators find tremendous opportunities in the region. They perceive these trends as signs of demand for the product they offer. This demand is found in the wealthier parts of the region and in the places, such as Vietnam and China, with the fastest-growing middle-classes. These places are fertile ground for the education businesses that were created in other parts of the world. The linkages with UK firms are the clearest.

The two classic cases are Nord Anglia and Cognita. Formed out of education reforms in the UK, Nord Anglia then began to operate international schools outside of Europe. In 2012, the firm shifted its headquarters to Hong Kong. This shift reflects the significance of Asia to the firm's operations. Out of 45 schools, 16 schools are located in Asia, and there are plans to open new international schools in the region.[1] Cognita kept its headquarters in the UK, but its expansion has been closely tied to Asia.

Conclusion

The origins of education businesses connect social, political, and economic trends in disparate parts of the globe. As transnational edu-businesses expanded and demand for international education grew in Asia, these firms came up against another set of challenges. The regulatory environment in many countries protected national education systems against private encroachment. The next two chapters examine the ways states responded when edu-businesses arrived at the door.

---

[1] The firm has 16 schools in Asia, 11 in Europe, 12 in the Americas, and 6 in the Middle East.

References

Au, W., & Hollar, J. (2016). Opting out of the education reform industry. *Monthly Review, 67*(10), 29–37.

BBC News. (2017 June 12). *Lilac sky academy trust's catalogue of 'irregularities'.* https://www.bbc.com/news/uk-england-40249763. Accessed August 8, 2018.

Brooks, R., & Waters, J. (2010). Social networks and educational mobility. *Globalisation, Societies and Education, 8*(1), 143–157.

Burch, P. (2009). *Hidden markets: the new education privatization.* New York: Routlege.

Cohan, W. D. (2017, May 2). Michael Milken invented the modern junk bond, went to prison, and then became one of the most respected people on Wall Street. *Business Insider.* https://www.businessinsider.com/michael-milken-life-story-2017-5/?IR=T Accessed June 27, 2018.

Collins, F. L. (2013). Regional pathways: Transnational imaginaries, infrastructures and implications of student mobility within Asia. *Asian and Pacific Migration Journal, 22*(4), 475–500.

Collins, F. L., Sidhu, R., Lewis, N., & Yeoh, B. S. A. (2014). Mobility and desire: International students and Asian regionalism in aspirational Singapore. *Discourse: Studies in the Cultural Politics of Education, 35*(5), 661–676.

Dickens, J. (2017, June 7). Accounts reveal shocking financial mismanagement at defunct academy trust. *Schools Week.* https://schoolsweek.co.uk/accounts-reveal-shocking-financial-mismanagement-at-defunct-academy-trust/. Accessed August 8, 2018.

Earley, P. (1998). *School improvement after inspection? School and LEA responses.* London: Sage.

Entrich, S. R. (2018). *Shadow education and social inequalities in Japan: Evolving patterns and conceptual implications.* New York: Springer.

Falk, M. L., & Graf, A. (2016). Introduction to the issue: Student mobility within Southeast Asia. *TRaNS: Trans -Regional and -National Studies of Southeast Asia, 4*(1), 1–5.

Glass, D. (2014). The international schools market: Data and details of a dynamic global market. Webinar. http://home.edweb.net/international-schools-marketdata-details-dynamic-global-market/. Accessed January 14, 2015.

Johnson, A. (2012, January 27). City of London academy hits bottom spot. *Islington Tribune.* http://archive.islingtontribune.com/news/2012/jan/city-london-academy-hits-bottom-spot. Accessed March 2, 2015.

Kim, Y. (2016). *Shadow education and the curriculum and culture of schooling in South Korea.* New York: Palgrave Macmillan.

Klein, N. (2008). *The shock doctrine: The rise of disaster capitalism.* Picador.

Lee, M., & Wright, E. (2016). Moving from elite international schools to the world's elite universities. *International Journal of Comparative Education and Development, 18*(2), 120–136.

Ma, Y., & Garcia-Murillo, M. A. (2018). *Understanding international students from Asia in American universities: Learning and living globalization.* Springer.

Mok, K. (2012). The rise of transnational higher education in Asia. *Higher Education Policy, 25*(2), 225–241.

Molnar, A. (2006). The commercial transformation of public education. *Journal of Education Policy, 21*(5), 621–640.

Olmedo, A. (2013). Policy-makers, market advocates and edu-businesses: New and renewed players in the Spanish education policy arena. *Journal of Education Policy, 28*(1), 55–76.

Pearson International Schools Community. https://community.pearsoninternationalschools.com/homepage. Accessed June 20, 2018.

Ridge, N. Y., Shami, S., & Kippels, S. (2016). Private education in the absence of a public option: The cases of the United Arab Emirates and Qatar. *Forum for International Research in Education, 3*(2), 41–60.

Roesgaard, M. H. (2006). *Japanese education and the cram school business: Functions, challenges and perspectives of the juku.* Copenhagen: NIAS Press.

Sahlgreen, G. H. (2010). Schooling for money: Swedish education reforms and the role of the profit motive. *Institute of Economic Affairs Discussion Paper, 33.* https://iea.org.uk/wp-content/uploads/

2016/07/Schooling%20for%20money%20-%20web%20version_0.pdf. Accessed March 28, 2018.

Saltman, K. J. (2005). *The Edison schools: Corporate schooling and the assault on public education.* New York: Routledge.

Seth, M. J. (2002). *Education fever: Society, politics, and the pursuit of schooling in South Korea.* Honolulu: University of Hawaii Press.

Sims, T. (2017, August 23). Frankfurt's international schools see Brexit bonus. *Reuters.* https://www.reuters.com/article/us-britain-eu-education/frankfurts-international-schools-see-brexit-bonus-idUSKCN1B30D3. Accessed December 4, 2017.

Singer, A. (2017, June 2). Pearson and the neo-liberal global assault on public education. *Huffington Post.* https://www.huffingtonpost.com/entry/pearson-and-the-neo-liberal-global-assault-on-public_us_592fe501e4b0d80e3a8a336c. Accessed January 14, 2018.

Smithers, R. (2005, February 4). Woodhead overrode inspectors to fail improving school. *The Guardian.* https://www.theguardian.com/uk/2005/feb/04/politics.freedomofinformation. Accessed March 13, 2015.

Srivastava, P., & Walford, G. (2016). Non-state actors in education in the Global South. *Oxford Review of Education, 42*(5), 491–494.

Verger, A., Lubienski, C., & Steiner-Khamsi, G. (2016). The emergence and structuring of the global education industry: Towards an analytical framework. In A. Verger, C. Lubienski, & G. Steiner-Khamsi (Eds.), *World yearbook of education 2016: The global education industry* (pp. 1–26). New York: Routledge.

Verger, A., Lubienski, C., & Steiner-Khamsi, G. (2017). The emerging global education industry: Analysing market-making in education through market sociology. *Globalisation, Societies and Education, 15*(3), 325–340.

Wallace, W. (2005, April 29). Who failed Islington Green? *TES Newspaper.* https://www.tes.co.uk/article.aspx?storycode=2095239. Accessed January 12, 2015.

Weale, S. (2015, June 10). 'It's a political failure': How Sweden's celebrated schools system fell into crisis. *The Guardian.* https://www.theguardian.com/world/2015/jun/10/sweden-schools-crisis-political-failure-education. Accessed May 5, 2018.

Wiborg, S. (2014, September 9). The big winners from Sweden's for-profit 'free' schools are companies, not pupils. *The Conversation.* https://theconversation.com/the-big-winners-from-swedens-for-profit-free-schools-are-companies-not-pupils-29929. Accessed December 3, 2017.

Wiborg, S. (2015). Privatizing education: Free school policy in Sweden and England. *Comparative Education Review, 59*(3), 473–497.

Wigmore, T. (2016, June 18). Why Sweden's free schools are failing. *NewStatesman.* https://www.newstatesman.com/politics/education/2016/06/why-sweden-s-free-schools-are-failing. Accessed February 15, 2018.

Chapter 4
Government Policies and the Shifting Place of International Schools in the Education System

International schools appear to form isolated islands in a country's education landscape. Traditionally, they have been so in many places. However, with the corporatization of international schools and efforts to attract local students, international schools have been brought into greater contact with local education policy. In many places, parents wish to send their children to an international school; those schools have been only too eager to pursue local students. These factors place a great deal of pressure on barriers separating national education systems from international schools. Governments have been forced to respond. Should international schools be separate from the education system? Or should they be incorporated into it? Should local students be allowed to attend? What defines "local" versus non-local students? States now grapple with these questions.

In this chapter, I outline ways that governments have responded to this new challenge. The responses have been diverse. The diversity relates to core aspects of these societies and their political systems. Access to international schools connects to fundamental questions of citizen rights and who qualifies for them. As a result, even the category of "international school" can take on distinct meanings. The lines between international school and "private school" can be clear or blurred, for example.

Responses to the question of whether nationals should be permitted to enter internationals schools lead to distinct models of how international schools relate to the education system. In one model, international schools fall into a broad category of private schools. That is, international schools are not regulated any differently from other private schools. In this school landscape, there are state schools and private schools, with international schools falling in the latter. This arrangement, which I call Model I, can mean that local students are permitted to attend international schools. In a second model, international schools for foreign students are distinguished from a private school industry that serves local students. In this school landscape, there

---

This chapter draws on Hyejin Kim and Erik Mobrand (2019), Stealth Marketisation: how international school policy is quietly challenging education systems in Asia, Globalisation, Societies and Education. The journal can be found at www.tandfonline.com.

© The Author(s), under exclusive license to Springer Nature Singapore Pte Ltd., part of Springer Nature 2019
H. Kim, *How Global Capital is Remaking International Education*,
SpringerBriefs in Education, https://doi.org/10.1007/978-981-32-9672-5_4

are state schools, private schools for locals, and international schools for foreigners. I call this Model II.

These two models are purely heuristic and are not necessarily followed precisely anywhere. Even within one country, aspects of one model may be seen at the primary level and another at the secondary level. These models are useful for making comparisons in the ways governments respond to the issue of making a dividing line between the national education system and the space transnational education firms can occupy.

In what follows, I examine states' responses to these questions. I focus here on the experiences of six countries that have recently adjusted their international school policies. These can be organized into three pairs. Each pair shares a common context or challenge. First, in the former British colonies of Malaysia and Singapore, managing ethnic pluralism is a key task for education policy. Second, in the democracies of Indonesia and South Korea, states have had to respond to affluent citizens opting out of public education. Third, in the post-socialist states of Vietnam and China, marketization of schooling—which occurred in the context of marketization of many spheres—quickly created a diversity of education opportunities and experiences.

Managing Difference and Inequality in Former British Colonies

The two states form a natural comparison. They have a shared history, and many common institutions and laws. International schools, several established in the early twentieth century, served the substantial British and expatriate populations. The colonial period also saw the founding of large numbers of private schools, which became the premier education institutions in both places.

A core issue facing the states since Singapore's formation as an independent state in 1965—when it separated from Malaysia—has been the handling of ethnic diversity. Malaysia has a Malay majority and a large Chinese minority and many Indians as well; Singapore is mostly Chinese but also has Malay and Indian populations. Managing this diversity has been a central challenge for education as for all aspects of politics. In Malaysia, ethnicity was made explicitly political, as a ruling Malay group, Barisan Nasional, maintained power for five decades until 2018 by making entitlements specific to Malays and other "sons of the soil" or *bumiputra*. English was abandoned as an official school language in favor of Malay. In Singapore, by contrast, the priority of being global dominated. English became the medium of education, and Chinese medium schools were suppressed. In the name of preserving racial harmony, Singapore's rulers—also continuous since independence—have banned speech and organization that could stir up communal tensions.

Malaysia

International schools in Malaysia should be understood in the broader context of racial politics and private education. In this multiethnic nation, Chinese (with nearly one-third of the population) and Indians are excluded from many benefits. Education is one sphere where *bumiputra* receive privileges. Due to these policies, public education institutes have favored Malays and aboriginal communities. University admissions policies also give priority to *bumiputra*. Private education, from primary through tertiary levels, serves these excluded, non-*bumiputra* Malaysians (Welch, 2011: 59). Older English-medium schools, as well as Chinese-language schools, have persisted to cater to these populations. Ethnic policy in essence created space for private educational institutions to grow. In other words, the national education system is an exclusive one that encourages many to turn to private options.

In this system, international schools are treated as a type of private school in Malaysia. Private schools, in turn, have contained two categories, international schools and independent Chinese high schools. Most regulations on international schools have been the same as those for private schools more broadly. A rule specific to international schools was, until 2012, that the proportion of Malaysian students at each school should not exceed 40%.

Any barrier between international schools and other private schools came crashing down in 2012. In that year, two key policies were shifted. First, the government abandoned an attempt to make English the compulsory language for teaching mathematics and science, a policy that had been introduced in 2003. The logic behind that policy had been to improve most people's English language ability. Then-prime minister Mahathir bin Mohamad argued that with better English skills, young Malaysians would become more employable. The pressures of globalization led to greater demand for English-speaking people (Mandal, 2000: 1002, 1011; Yang & Ishak, 2012: 452). According to some research, poor English contributed to a high unemployment rate at that time (Chan & Tan, 2006: 309; Yang & Ishak, 2012: 452). However, the policy did not help. By 2012 it was clear that teaching mathematics and science in English was leading to poor results in those subjects. Only some 28% of students recorded a minimum score in a national English examination in 2011 (Malaysia Education Blueprint 2013–2025, 2013: 33). For this reason, the government retreated from the policy. As a result, families wishing for their children to continue with an English-language education would have to look beyond the public education system.

A second policy shift in 2012 was the lifting of the 40% limit on places for Malaysians at international schools. Instead, international schools could admit as many Malaysian children as they wished. In combination with the withdrawal of mandatory teaching of mathematics and science in English, this policy unleashed tremendous interest in international schools among Malaysian families. These schools had been growing, the government was turning away from teaching in English, and now there was no legal barrier to attending international schools. Especially for parents who had experienced difficulty finding work due to poor English skills, this confluence of changes gave them a good reason to give international schools a hard look.

The effect was instant. In 2013, the number of Malaysian students in the country's 126 international schools surpassed the foreign students. In 2012, 15,000 Malaysian children were studying in international schools; by 2017, the figure reached 39,161, according to official statistics from the Ministry of Education (MalaysianDigest.com, 2015; *New Straits Times*, 2017). The number of international schools quickly exceeded the number planned by the Malaysian government: state plans set 87 schools as the goal by 2020 but by 2017 there were already nearly 50% more than that figure. These schools were supposed to teach 75,000 students by 2020, but by 2017 already 61,156 were enrolled (*New Straits Times*, 2017; Yang & Ishak, 2012). Malaysian students now outnumber foreign students two to one in international schools. While government plans intended international schools to attract students from overseas, the result has been to see Malaysians shift into international schools.

International school policy in Malaysia relates directly to the education system as a whole. Authorities have permitted, even encouraged, the international schools to take on parts of the education system. The meaning of "international school" is thus more like a private school rather than one serving an expatriate population. Malaysia today stands as an example of Model I education system. The division between local schools and international schools is not sharp.

Singapore

As a "world city" hosting the offices of multinational corporations, Singapore has a substantial expatriate population and numerous international schools. In the past ten years, the international school landscape has expanded greatly. Schools previously serving families from a particular nation have shifted to offer "international" programs. The German School thus became the German European School. The large international school operators have moved in as well, taking over some of these schools. For example, UK-based Cognita acquired the Australian International School. These shifts de-link international schools from the communities they were once affiliated with and make them more attractive to a wider range of families.

State efforts that divide international schools from the national education system are rooted in the historical development of education in the city-state. Singapore inherited an education landscape with many private schools, especially for the majority Chinese community. These schools were pillars of Chinese communities (Visscher, 2007). After independence, the ruling People's Action Party was concerned that these schools could serve as a political base for an alternative elite. The establishment of English-medium government schools worked to decimate Chinese schools; the forced merging of the Chinese-medium Nanyang University into the National University of Singapore in 1980 dealt the last blow to Chinese education in the city-state. While the state has more recently allowed for "independent" junior colleges operated by private foundations, they remain governed by the Ministry of Education and for-profit bodies are prohibited in this sector. The elimination of Chinese schools also served the social and economic plans of the leadership. Since the republic's establishment in 1965, the state has made education a crucial instrument for the country's economic success. A common argument, for example, was that being an island with no natural resources, the human resources of the population represent Singapore's best economic hope (Lee, 2011). As "human resources," citizens should be cultivated in a way that makes them useful to the Singapore economic project. Education has a major role to play in this task. A component was to make English the main language of education, so that the environment would be attractive to multinational corporations. In these ways, constructing a national education system was a core political project. Unlike in Malaysia, there was no space for Singapore schools operating independently.

Singaporean students are largely tied to the main education system and do not have access to international schools. Students holding Singapore passports are barred from registering for international schools, except in special situations when permission is granted by the Ministry of Education. This regulation draws a clear line separating international schools from the rest of the education system. The only blurring of this line is in three international schools operated by local schools. In these schools, Singaporeans are permitted to attend.

There are thus two main forces keeping the international school space and local students separate. First, state policy has prevented most international schools from admitting Singaporean children. This policy builds on the history of the state reigning in control over private education. Second, because mainstream education has long been internationally-oriented, and mostly in English, international schools are less distinctive in this context. Even where Singaporeans can attend international schools, there has not been a rush to do so. The Singapore curriculum is itself based on what was inherited from the British. Singapore students take GCSEs. The education ministry has also kept up with international trends, and assimilated IB pedagogy through "integrated programs" provided by three elite independent schools. In the local school landscape, there is thus a substantial degree of internationalization. For those aspiring for academic success, an international school may not be particularly desirable. There already are well-worn paths from local schools to the world's most prestigious universities. Moreover, these paths are precisely what have defined Singapore's elite.

Singapore has anticipated and evaded the challenges of an expanding international school landscape. The authorities have managed to allow international schools to grow, while ensuring that they have minimal impact on the education system. The compromise of allowing three local schools to establish international branches has done little to impinge on the integrity of the national system. The contrast with Malaysia is stark. While Malaysia has made racial difference a founding point of education policy, Singapore has stressed equality and nation-building. In the former, international schools bled into the private system, whereas Singapore erected strong barriers. It should be pointed out that Singapore's policies do not stem from an aversion to education commercialization in principle. Many aspects of education in Singapore have been commercialized, including especially early education, supplementary programs, tertiary education, and vocational institutes. In international education, the state has actively courted transnational education firms to enter the country. However, these moves have been accompanied by careful management of the boundary between international schools and other parts of the education system.

Defining Citizenship and Legitimizing Differences in Democracies

In two of the region's democracies, the challenge has been different. Both have national education systems that integrate the population. However, in the face of economic liberalization, both have seen students leave public education in pursuit of private, internationally-oriented education opportunities. The problem then has been to preserve families' rights to choose versus protection of the national education system.

South Korea

In South Korea, the education system has traditionally been tightly controlled by the Ministry of Education. While private schools exist, they remain subject to national rules. The central government dispatches teachers and sets the curriculum. The control is such that nobody has an option to leave the public school system. This is done in the name of fairness and patriotism, and it represents the opposite end of the spectrum from Malaysia. The notion of fairness is taken seriously. Any illicit benefit is an outrage against a system that is fair for all. In one episode, an incident in which 15 students gained admission to reputable secondary schools through dubious means led to the dismissal of top officials, including the superintendent of schools for Seoul and the deputy education minister (Kang, 2004).

This control extended to who was eligible for international education. In the past, international schools were limited strictly to the children of non-Koreans; regulations prevented Koreans from attending them. This segmentation was effective. However, in the 2000s, many families started sending their children overseas for their primary and secondary education. In many cases, mothers and children would move to a destination with desirable schools while the "wild goose fathers" stay behind and earn income. In other instances, the child is packed off to live with a legal guardian matched through a middleman. Officials argued that the departure of so many children represented a loss of funds for the country. The government sought to find ways to encourage these students to return and see their schooling out in Korea.

The state did not simply open up international schools to Korean citizens. Formally, the country resembles Model II, as private schools are clearly divided from

Defining Citizenship and Legitimizing Differences in Democracies 49

foreign schools. The country's policies seem to demonstrate a serious approach to preventing international schools from undermining national education. At the same time, though, the state has created regulations that allow a number of loopholes that permit Koreans to gain an international education in the country.

A source of these loopholes lies in the complicated legal categories that have been invented around international education. "Schools for foreigners" (*oegugin haggyo*) are schools that can admit only students with foreign passports. However, following legislation passed in 2009, if a Korean national has been abroad for three years, he or she is permitted to attend one of these schools. These schools can negotiate with the education bureau to admit a larger proportion of Korean students, up to 50% of the student body. Another category is the "foreign education institution" (*oeguk gyoyuk gigoan*). These are schools operated by a foreign corporate body. These institutions are permitted to establish schools in specific places, such as free trade zones and US army bases. Any Korean may attend these schools, regardless of time spent abroad. However, Korean students at a school can occupy no more than 30% of the student body.[1] The purpose of introducing this category was to make it easier for foreign businessmen to find schools for their children. Due to these more relaxed restrictions, several new foreign schools have been established.

School investors have sought to take advantage of the new complexity in the legal regime. Scandals surrounding two international chains offer examples. Dulwich College Seoul (DCS) is part of a family of Dulwich schools, which started in the UK. The managers of DCS operated the school through a charitable entity established in Hong Kong. Doing so allowed the school to obtain preferential treatment from Seoul Metropolitan Government as a nonprofit entity. Meanwhile, revenue was diverted back to a for-profit entity, Dulwich College Management International, Ltd., registered in the Cayman Islands. The scheme was uncovered and DCS was investigated for embezzlement. Dwight School Seoul (DSS) also belongs to a larger group of schools. In the United States, Dwight Schools are for-profit firms. DSS is managed by a charitable foundation registered in Canada, again allowing the managers to enjoy benefits from Seoul. DSS became embroiled in a counterfeit foreign passport scandal (Kim, 2016; Yoo, 2012). The rules seem to have encouraged opportunistic individuals to hide behind legal registrations in order to gain benefits from public offices and generate quick revenues.

In another special zone, further loopholes are available to exploit. The provincial government on Jeju Island has greater autonomy than other local governments. It established a zone for international schools. Four new international schools were built and there is no limit on the percentage of Korean students who may enroll. These schools are expressly for Korean children, including those who have been abroad as well as those who were previously studying in Seoul. One source indicates that "24 out of 100 Korean students in Jeju international schools are from Kangnam," the Seoul district associated most with expensive education (Ku, 2014). Legislation No. 189-4 for Jeju Special Autonomous Province explains that "international schools"

---

[1] Article 10 of the Regulations on the Establishment and Operation of Schools and Kindergartens for Foreigners, revised July 26, 2016.

50 4 Government Policies and the Shifting Place of International …

are significant for strengthening foreign language ability and raise internationalized talent for the future. This policy contradicts the overall requirement that Korean children should participate in national education. Koreans who can afford it clearly have options to leave the national school system and pursue an international education.

In the South Korean example, a rigid barrier has apparently been erected between what are essentially private schools and schools for foreign students. The country's policies demonstrate a serious approach to preventing international schools from undermining national education. On the other hand, though, the rules now allow a section of wealthier Korean families to send their children to expensive, non-Korean schools. This move has implications for national identity as well as for equality. These wealthier families can use their wealth to carve out a distinct education path for their children, one that is sanctioned by the state. Further, these families choose to remove their children from a national education program. Students do not learn Korean history and instruction is done in English. These features mean that international schools are not training students as engaged Koreans, but as detached "global" citizens.

Indonesia

In Indonesia, the longest-running international schools once served families of the Dutch colonial elite. These schools have since been brought into the global circuit of international schools. For example, the Netherlands Inter-community School in Jakarta, established in 1967, is now operated by Hong Kong-based Nord Anglia Education. Further, the number of international schools grew tremendously in the early 2000s, as many Indonesian children began studying in them.

Concerned that international schools were growing quickly while charging high fees and offering questionable education, the state made new regulations. As education ministry spokesman Ibnu Hamad stated, "the intention of the regulation was to weed out low-quality schools that charge a premium by adding 'international' to their name" (Maulia & Khalik, 2014). It corresponds to Hayden's point that international schools prefer to use 'international' in order to be more competitive than others (Hayden, 2006:10). In 2014, a law was passed that introduced a distinction among international schools. As in South Korea, the distinction was between schools for foreign nationals and schools for citizens. Since 2015, when the law came into force, schools linked to foreign entities, usually embassies, are governed by one set of rules and other "international" schools by another.[2] Only foreign passport holders can attend the former, while Indonesian citizens are permitted to attend the latter.

---

[2]There are other examples. The British International School was established in 1974 and the British and Australian embassies were founding members. The school still invites two Council members. But they also changed the name to the British Intercultural School. The Australian Independent School is a foreign entity and non-profit organization. It accepts foreign passport holders who are interested in receiving an Australian education.

Defining Citizenship and Legitimizing Differences in Democracies 51

A more stringent set of laws now governs this latter category. A first is that none could use the word "international" in the school name. The reasoning was that the term had become little more than a slogan for attracting students. Any private school would begin calling itself "international" and that label would be good for its marketing. After this word was not permitted, schools had to change their names. Jakarta International School, for instance, became Jakarta Intercultural School. In addition, all schools, with the exception of foreign-operated schools, should provide instruction on Indonesian culture and language. In these international schools, Indonesians thus retain connections to their country. Students even take national examinations, just like their compatriots in other schools, after the sixth, ninth, and twelfth grades of school. The policy has led to criticism that Indonesian graduates would be behind in "an increasingly globalized world" (Jakarta Globe, 2014).

In terms of ownership structure, foreign nationals or enterprises can own up to 49% of a school. Full foreign ownership is no longer possible. Local entities can collaborate with foreigners in arrangements called collaborative education units (Satuan Pendidikan Kerjasama, or SPKs). By 2015, there were 195 English-medium international schools, of which 75 were located in Jakarta (Relocate Global, 2018).

Indonesia and South Korea have faced similar challenges in making international school policy. Both have opted for a response more in line with Model II than Model I, as outlined above. In both places, a proportion of families have opted out of the public school system, either by moving overseas or by attending international schools in the country. Concerned that these trends can undermine the school system as a site of socialization and national integration, and can also exacerbate inequality, authorities have sought to limit access to international schools. Neither has aimed to eliminate local attendance at such schools, but both have introduced new distinctions between foreign-oriented schools for citizens and non-citizens. These policies represent an effort to accept a degree of the outward shift of students, while attempting to re-impose boundaries on the national education system.

Protecting National Identity and Empowering Markets in Post-socialist Contexts

For the post-socialist states of China and Vietnam, cost-based differences in education opportunities are a more recent phenomenon. Any international education institutions were strictly for foreign diplomats; no private education system existed. As those societies became more commercial, marketization also crept into education. Emerging private schools became blended with international schools, and foreign populations demanding international schools also increased. Vietnam and China therefore had similar situations to respond to in dealing with their international schools. In particular, international school expansion raised the question of the extent to which the affluent population would be permitted to gain an education separate from the education system which serves as a central means of socialization into the nation.

Vietnam

A variety of internationally-oriented education institutions have opened in Vietnamese cities in the past decade, and Vietnamese families show a great interest in them. In response, the state has re-written its regulations on international schools. Foreign-invested schools can enroll only a limited number of Vietnamese citizens. Bilingual schools comprise another category of the schools. These schools offer classes in English or another foreign language, in addition to Vietnamese, and they also use components from the Vietnamese education curriculum. As long as these components are included, local students are permitted to attend bilingual schools. The compromise here shares features with Indonesia, where local attendance at international schools is contingent on elements of the national curriculum and language being used.

Until 2018, Decree 73/2012/ND-CP ("Decree 73") governed foreign-invested schools. This law was considered a hurdle to gaining education investment from foreign investors (*The Pie News*, 17 May 2017). In February 2017, the Vietnamese Ministry of Education and Training introduced a revised draft decree. The revised regulation, which went into effect in August 2018 as "Decree 86" (formally, Decree 86/2018/ND-CP), favors foreign capital in education. A major revision is the raising of the cap on Vietnamese nationals in foreign-invested schools. Previously, under Decree 73, children with Vietnamese nationality could account for up to ten per cent of the students in foreign-invested primary and middle schools, and 20 per cent in foreign-invested high schools (Conventus Law, 2017). Now, under Decree 86, up to 50 per cent of students in each foreign-invested school can be Vietnamese. The motive for the revision is similar to that in South Korea: according to Phan Manh Hung, the attorney who assisted the Ministry of Education and Training to draft the new decree, the government should encourage Vietnamese students not to move overseas for school (*The Pie News*, 17 May 2017). The Department of Overseas Training (under the Ministry of Education and Training) reports that 130,000 students were studying abroad in 2016, which represents an increase of 20,000 from the previous year (Vietnam Australia International School website, 2017). Studying at an international school in Vietnam is an alternative, one that is preferable in the government's view.

The profile of Phah Manh Hung, a lawyer tasked with drafted the policy revision, reveals the government's thinking on education. He comes from the foreign-invested education sector, so there should be no surprise that his revisions are friendly to foreign education businesses. In his recommendations, he emphasizes that education is a means of cultivating competitive talent for the global economy (Education Investor, 2017, July 17). Phah is an education policy entrepreneur. These are individuals who are "political actors that aim to promote new policy solutions among practice communities" (Verger, Fontdevila, & Zancajo, 2016: 141–142). He is a link between the international education industry and the re-making of education policy in Asia.

The Vietnamese state is caught between priorities of developing education as a sector, retaining students, and maintaining the integrity of the national school system. Policy appears shifting decisively toward marketisation of the education system through international schools. The nod toward protecting national identity will have little impact if the proposed lifting of quotas on Vietnamese students goes through. Decree 86 is one of the clearest vehicles of quiet marketization. The major international school groups have gained a foothold in Vietnam—Nord Anglia acquired a set of four British schools in 2015—and their interest in the country is surely related more to the local population than the foreign one.

In Vietnam, then, a rapid shift occurred from a closed system in which international schools were only for non-citizens to one with few boundaries. Increasingly, international schools serve Vietnamese who can afford them. Families choose to opt out of the normal education system. This trend will likely have implications for the school system and for society. If the affluent avoid the school system, then it can lose support. Meanwhile, a generation of foreign-oriented Vietnamese children is growing up with weaker understandings of their own society and language.

China

Private education has expanded rapidly in China since the 1990s. Basic government policy on who can attend international schools has been strict, but demand from parents for internationally-oriented education has also been massive. China's population is young relative to the wealthier parts of the region. Parents have also demonstrated a willingness to invest in their children's education in various ways and at increasingly young ages. International education opportunities are attractive to affluent parents. Besides the content of the education, the packaging of the schools increases their appeal. International schools can be luxurious, a fact that is reflected in fees. Some schools boast facilities that can be highly desirable. In Beijing, for example, air pollution is a constant concern for parents. The International School of Beijing responded by encasing its premises in a pressurized $5 million dome with air filtration (*CBS News*, 2013, July 17). Such an arrangement serves as a physical manifestation of the school's exclusivity. These pressures set the stage for transnational education enterprises to enter China and navigate regulations.

The basic regulation is that international schools owned by Chinese can admit Chinese nationals as pupils (Gaskell, 2017). Foreign-invested schools cannot enroll Chinese children. However, at the secondary level, foreign-invested schools can take in local students. These rules create space for international schools to enter and cater to Chinese families. According to the International Schools Consultancy, in 2016, 550 international schools were registered in China and 440 of them could admit local students. In these schools, more than 150,000 Chinese nationals gain an international education (Chong, 2016).

There are four types of schools in China's international education landscape. The first are expatriate schools, officially called schools for children of foreign workers (SCFW). These provide international education for foreign families living in China and Chinese who hold foreign passports. Chinese nationals are forbidden from attending these schools. Examples of such schools include Dulwich College, Wellington College, International School of Beijing, and Concordia International School. A second category are Sino-foreign cooperative schools. These are joint ventures, often involving transnational education firms, and they can be established only at the secondary level. The Chinese owner provides land and financial investment, while the foreign firm brings soft investment, such as the curriculum. Chinese students can enter this second type of international school (Yang, 2011).

Transnational education firms are thus able to enter China in an indirect way. A good example is United World College Changshu, which opened in 2015. Chinese UWC alumni who studied in school branches in Norway, Canada, and Hong Kong worked together to build the school; these founders serve as chairman and board members of the school. Officially, this is a Sino-foreign joint venture, and it can admit Chinese secondary school students. UWC is the foreign partner, but the UWC representatives are Chinese. UWC China even received IB status (on May 8, 2015) before its grand opening (on Nov. 7, 2015), when most schools must wait years for that status. The joint venture scheme in this case is a way for a transnational school chain to enter China and enroll local students.

Bilingual schools comprise a third category. These offer both Chinese and international programs. This type of school has no limit on attendance by Chinese nationals. They usually offer internationally recognized diplomas, such as IB and IGCSE. These schools primarily enroll local children. State schools make up the fourth type of international school. Many publicly-operated schools run connected international schools, open for local students, at the upper secondary level.

Despite regulations, none of these types of schools can be seen as entirely separate from serving the local population. Even though the SCFWs cannot admit local students, SCFW-operators—often education transnationals—see these schools now as part of a bigger strategy to appeal to local students, who represent a far larger "market." First, these firms establish an international school for foreigners. Then, on the basis of the reputation received from that school, they open a school for Chinese. For example, Dulwich College began by setting up schools for which only foreign children were eligible. As the brand gained reputation and experience in the country, it moved on to cooperate with Chinese schools. In this cooperation, Dulwich supplies international education components to the local schools. Two schools in Suzhou and Zhuhai offer British curricula to Chinese students thanks to the assistance of Dulwich.[3]

---

[3]This information comes from the websites of Dulwich International High Schools in Zhuhai and Suzhou.

Conclusion

Across Asia, states are under pressure to allow their citizens to enter corporatized, internationally-oriented education programs. In places such as Malaysia, the state has done little to protect the education system from transnational education firms offering international education. Elsewhere, varying degrees of protection have been insisted upon, but usually with some compromise being made. South Korea's encouragement of transnational education firms opening international schools—for which Korean students who have a few years of overseas experience are eligible—is an example of such compromise. Even these compromises raise questions about the future of national education systems.

Policies on who can attend international schools are a crucial component to the viability of transnational education firms. Moreover, through this issue, international school policy has become a major component of mainstream education policy in Asia. Policies on international schools relate not just to expatriate families but to the viability of national education systems. These policies have seen tremendous flux in recent years as pressures from school operators and parents have forced states to adjust. While responses vary, in all of the countries discussed here, the state leaves at least one door open for international schools to enter and admit local students. There are increasing opportunities for affluent families in the region to send their children to for-profit international schools. If this trend continues, what does it mean for the future of the elite in Asia? What does it mean for investment in public education systems? What will the implications be for the national solidarity that public education systems can bring? These are some of the crucial questions emerging from shifts in policies on international schools.

References

CBS News. (2013, July 17). *Beijing pollution forces students to play under dome.* https://www.cbsnews.com/news/beijing-pollution-forces-students-to-play-under-dome/. Accessed January 5, 2018.

Chan, S. H., & Tan, H. (2006). English for mathematics and science: Current Malaysian language-in-education policies and practices. *Language and Education, 20*(4), 306–321.

Chong, K. (2016, September 24). *The Straits Times.* http://www.straitstimes.com/asia/east-asia/boom-time-for-international-schools. Accessed July 12, 2018.

Conventus Law. (2017, July 10). *Vietnam: New draft decree on foreign cooperation and investment in education.* http://www.conventuslaw.com/report/vietnam-new-draft-decree-on-foreign-cooperation/. Accessed July 12, 2018.

Education Investor. (2017, July 17). Expansion for Vietnam.

Gaskell. R. (2017, May 9). Dragon in the Box. *International Teacher Magazine.* http://consiliumeducation.com/itm/2017/05/09/dragon-in-the-box/. Accessed July 12, 2018.

Hayden, M. (2006). *Introduction to international education: International schools and their communities.* London: SAGE.

Jakarta Globe. (2014, December 1). http://jakartaglobe.id/news/new-school-regulation-quality-drop-along-international/. Accessed July 12, 2018.

Kang, J. (2004). *Hanguk hyeondaesa sanchaek 1960, vol 3. (Modern history of Korea, the 1960s)*. Inmulgoasasangsa.

Kim, Y. (2016). *Shadow education and the curriculum and culture of schooling in South Korea*. New York: Palgrave Macmillan.

Ku, Y. (2014, September 28). From Gangnam, 24 out of 100 Koreans in international schools in Jeju Island (in Korean). *Ohmynews*. http://www.ohmynews.com/NWS_Web/View/at_pg.aspx? CNTN_CD=A0002037898. Accessed June 19, 2018.

Lee, K. J. (2011). The semiotics of Singapore's founding myths of multiracialism and meritocracy. *The American Sociologist, 42*(2), 261–275.

MalaysianDigest.com. (2015, May 19). Malaysian parents choose international schools over national schools.

Malaysia Education Blueprint 2013–2025. (2013). *Ministry of Education*. http://planipolis.iiep. unesco.org/sites/planipolis/files/ressources/malaysia_blueprint.pdf. Accessed August–September 2017.

Mandal, S. K. (2000). Reconsidering cultural globalization: The English language in Malaysia. *Third World Quarterly, 21*(6), 1001–1012.

Maulia, E., & Khalik, A. (2014, December 4). With rules hazy, international schools in Indonesia are left in confusion. *Jakarta Globe*. http://jakartaglobe.id/news/rules-hazy-international-schools-indonesia-left-confusion/. Accessed June 10, 2018.

New Straits Times. (2017, April 28). Malaysian parents pinched by rising international school fees.

Relocate Global. (2018, January 29). *The changing face of international education in Indonesia*. https://www.relocatemagazine.com/articles/education-schools-the-changing-face-of-international-education-in-indonesia-apac1. Accessed July 12, 2018.

The Pie News. (2017, May 17). Vietnam: local enrolments at foreign schools expected to grow after cap removed. https://thepienews.com/news/vietnam-local-enrolments-foreign-schools-to-grow-cap-removed/. Accessed July 12, 2018.

Verger, A., Fontdevila, C., & Zancajo, A. (2016). *The privatization of education: A political economy of global education reform*. New York: Teachers College Press.

Vietnam Australia International School. (2017, July 14). *International school or international bilingual school? Considering the students' outcomes and family finances*. https://www.vas.edu.vn/en/post/chon-truong-quoc-te-hoan-toan-hay-song-ngu. Accessed July 12, 2018.

Visscher, S. (2007). *The business of politics and ethnicity: A history of the Singapore Chinese Chamber of Commerce and Industry*. Singapore: NUS Press.

Welch, A. (2011). *Higher education in Southeast Asia: Blurring borders, changing balance*. London: Routledge.

Yang, H. (2011). International schools in China amid globalization and marketization of education. *Social Studies Education, 50*(2), 117–132.

Yang, L., & Ishak, S. A. (2012). Framing controversy over language policy in Malaysia: The coverage of PPSMI reversal (teaching of mathematics and science in English) by Malaysian newspapers. *Asian Journal of Communication, 22*(5), 449–473.

Yoo. S. (2012, October 13). D international school being involved with illegal admission (in Korean). *Chosun Ilbo*. http://news.chosun.com/site/data/html_dir/2012/10/13/2012101300726. html?Dep0=twitter&d=2012101300726. Accessed February 2018.

Chapter 5
Economic Planning, Education Policy, and International Schools

The expansion of transnational education corporations (TECs) might be viewed as the natural consequence of globalization. As demand for international school opportunities increases, there is perhaps little surprise that firms stepped in to provide those opportunities. Such a view misses the centrality of the state to the creation of markets for international education. As Stephen Ball notes in relation to a range of education policy areas in the United Kingdom, the cause of the emergence of businesses for education policy "is not some kind of spontaneous neo-liberal free market, its dynamics have to be understood alongside the dynamics of and changes in the state itself and the role of the state in shaping industry behaviour and economic transactions" (Ball, 2009: 97). States in parts of Asia have not been passive bystanders as international schools have transformed into lucrative businesses. Rather, states have actively participated in the commercialization of international education. States have supported this commercialization in the pursuit of economic goals. International schools have thus become objects not just of education policy but also, even mainly, of economic policy.

Why have states supported international schools? What policy tools have states used to give such support? A central consideration in states' approaches to international schools is the drive to be competitive internationally. The push to make the economy stronger than another's shapes many policy areas in the region. International school policy should be understood in the context of this competition. The "competition state," oriented to strengthening the nation through economic performance, "has pursued increased marketization in order to make economic activities located within the national territory" (Cerny, 1997: 259). As Bob Jessop (2002) theorizes, the state has transformed into an agent of economic action. This economic purpose has transformed the state and affected a range of its activities. Writing on welfare regimes, for example, has noted that in East Asia's "productivist welfare regimes," the goal of production has subsumed welfare functions (Holliday, 2000). Such a position is a legacy of the state playing a pre-eminent role in the industrializing experience.

© The Author(s), under exclusive license to Springer Nature Singapore Pte Ltd., part of Springer Nature 2019
H. Kim, *How Global Capital is Remaking International Education*, SpringerBriefs in Education, https://doi.org/10.1007/978-981-32-9672-5_5

In this chapter, I examine the links between economic planning and the rise of transnational education firms in international education. Economic planning creates various opportunities and constraints for education businesses to enter. A central theme here is the transformation of international schools into a sector. This shift has occurred not just through firms taking advantage of states with lax regulation. Rather, the state has actively fostered and supported the creation of an international school sector. Here I offer examples from Malaysia and Singapore, where these linkages are clearest.

National Economic Competition and International School Growth

The creation of an international school sector is part of a global story of education becoming subject to economic forces. Such a trend has been observed in many areas, from growing commercialism in US schools (Saltman, 2005; Spring, 2015) to the World Bank's push for profit-driven schooling in Africa (Srivastava, 2016). International schools have not been immune to this trend. Two sets of competitive forces encourage states to allow education firms to open international schools. The first is competition for international firms to establish offices. Facilities for expatriates are central to this task, and international schools are a part of that. The second force is indirect: the cultivation of a "knowledge economy" has shifted education regulations to allow commercial education more generally, and this trend has had spillover effects in international schools.

I consider the first pressure first. This relates to the classic function of international schools: to serve the children of resident expatriates. The circumstances, though, have now changed, especially in major regional cities. Foreign residents are not in town by accident. Rather, foreign populations can be a symptom of incorporation into global economic competition. World cities now push hard to entice transnational corporations to establish offices. They desire global or regional headquarters to be set up. Global cities are highly responsive to this pressure. Hong Kong competes with Singapore for Asia offices, as Shanghai, Bangkok, and Kuala Lumpur also get in the mix. Dubai, Abu Dhabi, and Qatar battle it out in the Gulf. Competing to host such offices has become a core economic strategy of governments in these places.

In striving to compete, they have pursued many types of policies. Cutting corporate tax is among the most direct methods. They set up a good environment for firms. Having an environment attractive to expatriate families is part of this. If there are insufficient spaces in international schools or the schools have a poor reputation, then businesses will be reluctant to place their headquarters there.

Besides cites, zones with special economic regulations also host international schools. Several countries in the region have established economic zones where rules on international trade and/or investment are relaxed. In order to attract foreign staff and companies, authorities are keen to have international schools. I participated in one such project in China, where the government was eager to have major international education firms enter. A similar phenomenon can be found in places such as Cambodia, South Korea, and Malaysia.

As chains of international schools emerged, the question became not just whether international schools were sufficient in number and quality, but whether the best international schools were in town. If a competitor city had renowned international schools then it would not do to go without. This competitive logic has driven governments to embrace already recognized international school chains. The quality of the schools needs to be legible to a "global"—i.e., non-local—audience. And this is where established firms have an advantage. A good quality school in one place does not fit the bill. The purpose is to signal quality. Brands can do that.

The desire by governments to attract reputable school brands can even lead to highly dubious outcomes. In Seoul, South Korea, two international schools—Dulwich College and Dwight School—opened in expensive locations. The Seoul Metropolitan Government was so eager to have these schools that it allowed them to pay only one to 1.5 per cent of the market rental price for their sites. Dulwich was later discovered to be involved in an embezzlement scheme. Government moves such as this one are difficult to justify on grounds of serving the public.

The second pressure is indirect, and relates to a wider set of places than the "global cities" or special economic zones. Here the goal is to encourage economic activities that are tied to knowledge and knowledge production. Such activities are viewed as more desirable than simpler manufacturing tasks. Leaders of regions that have already established industrial bases wish to push toward developing a "knowledge economy." Such an economy requires "human resources" with the rights skills. This need means that there should be investment in education, especially in technical subjects as well as in English for communicating with global partners.

From the late 1990s, Singapore sought to make the "knowledge economy" a focal point of economic development plans. This plan meant investing heavily in research and development, including in industries such as biotechnology. It also meant turning Singapore into an "education hub," an endeavor that was simultaneously aimed at feeding into research and development activities and a sector for growth in itself. The resources of a state accustomed to directing efforts for economic development were shifted into education and research (Koh & Chong, 2014; Mok, 2008). Government agencies assist by making land available, facilitating contacts, and granting permissions for exchange and joint-degree programs. Both Singapore and neighboring Malaysia have made conscious efforts to mobilize international linkages in education for developmental purposes (Lai & Maclean, 2011; Lewis, 2011; Sidhu & Kaur, 2011). The Global Schoolhouse project, launched in 1998, has seen foreign universities enter Singapore, has brought tens of thousands of international students to the city's varsities, and has linked local higher education bodies to industry (Daquila, 2013; Olds, 2007; Pak & Tan, 2010; Sidhu, 2009; Sidhu, Ho, & Yeoh, 2011). The government agency in charge of promoting small and medium businesses identifies private education as an USD 2.2 billion "developing industry" and puts out information on running education businesses (SPRING website, https://www.spring.gov.sg/Developing-Industries/EDU/Pages/education.aspx).

For much of the region, there is an effort to develop technology. Innovations in technology are perceived as the way forward. This is as true for the post-industrial economies as it is for the industrial economies. They create industrial and technology parks. They hire researchers. For all of these tasks, training is necessary. They have thus focused on developing skills as a sector of the economy.

Promoting International Schools in Order to Compete: Singapore

As a global financial hub, Singapore places a priority on attracting and retaining foreign businesses. Sustaining a large population of foreign residents is presented as a human resources need (Ge & Ho, 2011). This logic has motivated the state to subject international schools to economic planning. Some of the most relevant policies on international schools come not from the education bureaucracy but from economic planners. A surge in the expatriate population occurred in the mid-2000s, as the number of non-citizen residents expanded from just over one million to 1.8 million between 2000 and 2010, in a total population of five million (Department of Statistics Singapore, 2017: 11). By this time, Singapore was promoting its knowledge economy and, overseas, global edu-businesses were emerging. The conditions were ripe for the entry of TECs into Singapore's international school sector. The overseas edu-businesses found Singapore attractive not only for the local opportunities but as a launching pad for gaining exposure to other Asian education "markets." The economic bureaucracies, too, were eager to find a way for coping with the influx.

A major theme in planning for international schools is competition with other global cities like Dubai or Hong Kong. Planners believe that attracting top schools is necessary for convincing multinational firms to stay in or come to Singapore. Alvin Tan, assistant managing director of the Economic Development Board (EDB) and chair of the Request-for-Interest (RFI) committee, points out that "Availability of quality schools for children of international executives is a key consideration when they decide on a posting location. Foreign schools play a part in strengthening Singapore's position as an attractive global city and home for business" (quoted in Philomin, 2015). This position is echoed by EDB's head of "human capital," who states that foreign schools are crucial for bringing overseas business to Singapore (Yang, 2017). Mr. Marcus Dass, director of human capital at EDB, said "foreign system schools have a role in strengthening Singapore's position as an attractive global city and home for business" (Ibid.).

In response to—and also anticipation of—expatriate population growth, the government led commercialization in the international school sector. One response was to actively develop commercial international schools. In 2004, the Ministry of Education (MOE) encouraged three local schools to establish affiliated international schools. Those three new international schools, one of which has its principal appointed by the MOE, began operations soon after. They are permitted to set and collect fees from students (Davie, 2015). This creates a sort of segmentation in the education landscape. These three schools' tuition fees are as expensive as other international schools. They embrace local Singaporean students and expats, and they all provide the International Baccalaureate program. They are affiliated with local elite independent schools that provide an integrated program that is composed of a six years program from grade 7 to 12, emphasizing a holistic approach and using IB. A interviewee, one of the graduate from the local independent schools said that the affiliated international categorized schools are for the locals who are not able to be accepted to local independent schools, but have wealthy parents (interview, September 2017).

Another state response was to actively support TECs. The most fundamental policy for attracting transnational edu-businesses in Singapore has been the selective opening of land and facilities for use as international schools. State control of land gives the government the ability to manage the number of international schools. Most land in Singapore was nationalized in the 1960s. Occupants usually purchase rights to land for a fixed period of tenure, often 99 years in the case of residential property and far shorter for schools. Aspiring school operators must bid on a facility or plot of land when the Economic Development Board (EDB) makes one available for an international school. This fact means that the EDB rather than the MOE is the main player in shaping international schools. In 2008, recognizing that international schools should continue to grow, the EDB institutionalized the process for allocating land for this purpose. It established a Request-for-Interest (RFI) exercise, run by an inter-agency committee. In this exercise, held every two or three years, the EDB announces land or facilities available for international schools and accepts bids for the space.

The RFI is the single clearest linkage between government policy and the entrance and growth of TECs. The winners of the RFI exercises point to this linkage. Cognita won the first bidding in 2008 for the Stamford American International School. Prior to this school, Cognita specialized in acquiring schools. This continues to be the only school worldwide that the firm has built. This suggests that the Singapore policy was instrumental in encouraging Cognita to shift strategy and develop a new school. In 2010, GEMS Education and Dulwich College made winning bids. This outcome brought both of these international chains to the city-state for the first time. Two homegrown providers, GIIS and OFS, won bids in 2012, permitting them to expand their campuses. While OFS remains relatively small, GIIS has expanded both in Singapore and overseas with branches in the UAE and elsewhere. In 2015, the Taylor Group's Nexus won the RFI (Nexus International School, 2015). Thus, major transnational edu-businesses have been the primary beneficiaries of this policy.

Building a "Knowledge Economy": Malaysia

Another route to fostering an international school sector comes through state efforts to make education a competitive component of the economy. Malaysia's experience illustrates this dynamic.

By the mid-1990s, Malaysia had gained attention for it fast-growing economy. Education, though, had not been commercialized. The country had maintained strict limits on private investment in education. Private education institutes and foreign universities were banned under a 1969 regulation. By 1995, when Malaysia's economy was peaking and the Petronas Towers were being completed, the country had no privately-invested universities (Welch, 2011: 65).

De-regulation in education—or, put another way, the construction of education as a sector—began in 1996. As Malaysia's economy internationalized, demands for a more skilled and English-speaking workforce grew. The state liberalized education in order to encourage the creation of education opportunities more suited to the country's shifting economic needs. The Private Higher Educational Institutional Act (PHEIA) of 1996 allowed private actors to invest in higher education (Yeoh, 2014: 210). Firms responded immediately to this opening. A dramatic increase in the number of private institutions followed; firms from other sectors even began setting up their own universities (Welch, 2011: 66). A wide range of actors became involved in the emerging education business: individual equity investors, private firms, consortia of companies, and public-private partnerships. Private tertiary institutions clustered in areas where multinational corporations were concentrated. An example is Penang, where firms in the electronics sector had established a significant presence (Yeoh, 2014: 216).

The Asian financial crisis of 1997–98 strengthened calls for a more internationally-oriented workforce. As unemployment rose, the government sought to improve Malaysians' competitiveness. Supporting the private education economy was a means toward this end. As in other parts of Asia, internationalizing was treated as the solution to the problems that caused the financial crisis. While Malaysian did not fully accept the IMF dogma on liberalization, in education we can see a move to privatize and open to international capital. Many multinational companies entered cities such as Kuala Lumpur and Penang. They needed a labor force that has specific skills, such as engineering and technologies. When the multinationals grew in Malaysia, private institutes geared toward delivering these skills emerged and were concentrated in the financial and industrial cities (Yeoh, 2014: 215–216).

While the stated purpose of education privatization was to make Malaysians more competitive in the global economy, once education became a business, the incentives shifted. Schools started recruiting students from overseas in a bid to increase their enrollments. Education groups actively enticed students from China, Indonesia, and Muslim countries in the Middle East and North Africa. Such students could find the opportunity in Malaysia attractive, especially for tertiary education. An effort to cultivate the skills of Malaysians thus quickly shifted to become an exercise in finding foreign "customers."

Building a "Knowledge Economy": Malaysia

These developments did not lead directly to invitations to set up international schools serving the primary and secondary ranges. However, the foundation was laid in the late 1990s for future developments. First, the privatization of universities and institutes made education into a business. Firms that grew in this area could—and in prominent cases, would—go on to build primary and secondary schools. Second, education was aimed partly at attracting foreign students. This move liked the private education business with service to international students. These developments set the basis for international school growth later.

A major expansion of international schools began in 2010. That year, the state outlined a set of National Key Economic Areas (NKEA) in a new Economic Transformation Program (ETP). These areas included agriculture, palm oil and rubber, and health care. Education was among the 12 designated areas. Through this plan, education became explicitly a sector for economic growth. Private school operators gained several benefits under the program. First, they are eligible for an investment tax allowance of 100% on qualifying capital expenditure within five years. Second, foreign ownership of international schools became permitted. Third, they could receive strong support from the government to obtain licenses and visas for expatriate teachers. These policies contributed to a jump in private schools and students. While only one percent of students in Malaysia were enrolled in private schools in 2002, 15 years later the figure reached 15% (*EI* July 17, 2017).

The state actively supports international schools. The Malaysian government oversaw the blueprint and it encouraged the establishment of international schools. The blueprint was contracted out to a big multinational consulting company. It suggested that the problem was underqualified teachers, and that foreign education experts could help improve the low scores in mathematics and science.

International education business circles are ecstatic over Malaysia's position on school liberalization. *Education Investor* magazine, the leading trade publication, heralds "Malaysia – a masterclass in private provision." The article touts the country's plan to "double export revenue through international education" by 2020 (Education Investor, 2017).

Conclusion

States in Asia have actively developed the international school landscape into a commercial sector. This has come about as a response to competitive pressures either to attract foreign business or to develop a knowledge economy that can compete internationally. The state has brought commercialism into education for this purpose. International schools are not marginal and they are not mainly educational concerns, they are economic concerns. This change is significant. In the next chapter, I move from the state to the education businesses themselves.

References

Ball, S. J. (2009). Privatising education, privatising education policy, privatising educational research: Network governance and the 'competition state'. *Journal of Education Policy, 24*(1), 83–99.

Cerny, P. G. (1997). Paradoxes of the competition state: The dynamics of political globalization. *Government and Opposition, 32*(2), 251–274.

Daquila, T. C. (2013). Internationalizing higher education in Singapore: Government policies and the NUS experience. *Journal of Studies in International Education, 17*(5), 629–647.

Davie, S. (2015, February 17). Home-grown international schools in demand from Singaporeans. *The Straits Times.* https://www.straitstimes.com/singapore/education/home-grown-international-schools-in-demand-from-singaporeans. Accessed December 8, 2017.

Department of Statistics Singapore (2017). *Yearbook of statistics Singapore.* https://www.singstat.gov.sg/-/media/files/publications/reference/yearbook_2017/yos2017.pdf. Accessed June 26, 2018.

Education Investor. (2017, July 17). Expansion for Vietnam.

Ge, Y., & Ho, K. (2011). Education and human capital management in a world city: The case of Singapore. *Asian Pacific Journal of Education, 31*(3), 263–276.

Holliday, I. (2000). Productivist welfare capitalism: Social policy in East Asia. *Political Studies, 48*(4), 706–723.

Jessop, B. (2002). *The future of the capitalist state.* Cambridge: Polity.

Koh, A., & Chong, T. (2014). Education in the global city: The manufacturing of education in Singapore. *Discourse: Studies in the Cultural Politics of Education, 35*(5), 625–636.

Lai, A., & Maclean, R. (2011). Managing human capital in world cities: The development of Hong Kong into an education hub. *Asia Pacific Journal of Education, 31*(3), 249–262.

Lewis, N. (2011). Political projects and micro-practices of globalising education: Building an international education industry in New Zealand. *Globalisation, Societies and Education, 9*(2), 225–246.

Mok, K. (2008). Singapore's global education hub ambitions. *International Journal of Education Management, 22*(6), 527–546.

Nexus International School. (2015, December 1). *Press release: Nexus International School secures RFI for new campus at Aljunied.* http://www.nexus.edu.sg/Downloads/Press.aspx. Accessed September 25, 2017.

Olds, K. (2007). Global assemblage: Singapore, foreign universities, and the construction of a 'global education hub'. *World Development, 35*(6), 959–975.

Pak, T. N., & Tan, C. (2010). The Singapore global schoolhouse: An analysis of the development of the tertiary education landscape in Singapore. *International Journal of Education Management, 24*(3), 178–188.

Philomin, L. (2015, April 28). More land parcels may be released to set up international schools. *Today Online.* https://www.todayonline.com/singapore/more-land-parcels-may-be-released-set-international-schools. Accessed December 12, 2017.

Saltman, K. J. (2005). *The Edison schools: Corporate schooling and the assault on public education.* New York: Routledge.

Sidhu, R. (2009). The brand name research university goes global. *Higher Education, 57*(2), 125–140.

Sidhu, G., & Kaur, S. (2011). Enhancing global competence in higher education: Malaysia strategic initiatives. *Journal of Higher Education in the Asia-Pacific, 36*(4), 219–236.

Sidhu, R., Ho, K. C., & Yeoh, B. (2011). Emerging education hubs: The case of Singapore. *Higher Education, 61*(1), 23–40.

Spring, J. (2015). *Economization of education: Human capital, global corporations, skill-based schooling.* New York: Routledge.

SPRING website. https://www.spring.gov.sg/Developing-Industries/EDU/Pages/education.aspx. Accessed September 26, 2017.

References

Srivastava, P. (2016). Questioning the global scaling up of low-fee private schooling: The nexus between business, philanthropy, and PPPs. In A. Verger, C. Lubienski, & G. Steiner-Khamsi (Eds.), *World yearbook of education 2016: The global education indistry* (pp. 248–263). New York: Routledge.

Welch, A. (2011). *Higher education in Southeast Asia: Blurring borders, changing balance*. London: Routledge.

Yang, C. (2017, April 19). School to be reused for expat students. *The Straits Times*. https://www.straitstimes.com/singapore/education/school-to-be-reused-for-expat-students. Accessed January 2018.

Yeoh, S. P. (2014). Entrepreneurs in private higher education: A case study of education entrepreneurs in a middle income economy. *International Educational Innovation and Public Sector Entrepreneurship, 23,* 209–249.

Chapter 6
The Business of International Education

International education does not have to be a business; for many schools, it still is not. Following the changes described in the previous chapters, a business of international education has developed. How does this business operate? How has corporatization changed international schools?

This line of inquiry relates to a wider question: What does corporatization do to schooling? Education researchers have been studying this problem for many years now. As the United States and United Kingdom, among other countries, moved to introduce privatizing reforms to their school systems, this issue gained focus. Free-market ideologues, often with the backing of conservative foundations, produced manifestos on the value of "school choice" reforms. Those arguments associate choice in schools with the liberties that individuals should have in a free society, as if freedom means nothing more than a sum of shopping decisions. This logic follows a political strategy of dubiously equating "free markets" with political freedom (Harvey, 2005: 7). Purported benefits of school markets include lower costs for operating schools and better performance as schools vie for students. Scholarship, on the other hand, points to a range of ways that markets alter education.

Creating education markets may not make schools better or more diverse. Instead, it might just make them work harder on their promotional activities. Lubienski (2005: 465) observes that school choice reforms in the United States encouraged firms to devote more energy and resources to marketing instead of actually trying to develop a different school experience: "Schools are not always responding to competitive incentives in the ways that the theory predicts." Research on universities, too, has found that competitive pressure has led not to improvements in teaching or research but to increased public relations activity (Baltodano, 2012: 500–01).

Corporatization can also alter the educational experience of children. When private vendors are invited to bid for school services, then students become exposed to or socialized in commercial culture at school. Such exposure can be as simple as vending machines in schools. Firms might sponsor school activities. Just as worrying, commercial textbook suppliers—which comprise some of the largest education-sector

---

© The Author(s), under exclusive license to Springer Nature Singapore Pte Ltd., part of Springer Nature 2019
H. Kim, *How Global Capital is Remaking International Education*, SpringerBriefs in Education, https://doi.org/10.1007/978-981-32-9672-5_6

firms—can introduce pedagogical material related to consumption. A common sort of example is the use of purchases of particular branded items as problems in mathematics textbooks. Saltman describes this as the "Cocacolonization" of education (Saltman, 2005). The concern is that the school is no longer a domain for cultivating membership in a civic community; rather, it is a training grounds for consumer capitalism.

These ideas can be related to international education, though we should bear in mind differences between international education and national education systems. International schools have always served groups that can pay fees, either out of pocket or through subsidies from employers. Concerns about access and equity resulting from corporatization have little relevance in this domain: they have traditionally been for the privileged. Still, effects of corporatization in international education bear a resemblance to what happens in other school contexts. My main theme here—and it is one that appears throughout this chapter—is that the business of education means an organization expends far greater energy on business than on education. This is not to say that the education offered is a poor quality, or is deficient in a particular way. My evidence does not come from results in terms of child development. Rather, I show how the organization of the business of education leads to an increase in energy devoted to activities that are peripheral to student outcomes.

This effect appears when examining the important questions about the international education business. These questions include the attraction of international education as a business, how firms in this field are organized, how they expand, how they appeal to parents, and who runs the schools.

Why Invest in International Education?

Several factors make education an attractive area for investment. First, education as a sector of business activity seems insensitive to economic cycles. The global financial crisis of 2007–08 did not lead to a downturn in education spending (IFC, 2010: 5). Households, at least in Asia, continued to spend on education. When jobs are scarce, turning to education or training is an alternative. This feature may even make education as a field of investment counter-cyclical. Second, education spending is strong and increasing in much of Asia. India, for example, is predicted to increase its spending on education from five to nine per cent of GDP between 2005 and 2025 (Ibid.). This is a sector with a growing consumer base.

A third consideration, more specific to international education, is rising inequality. Wealth disparities globally and within societies are among the most pressing issues of today. However, inequality is also an opportunity for investors in high-end schools. An IFC report shows that 18% of the worldwide 0–14 years-old population live in high-income families, while 25% come from upper middle income backgrounds, 28% from lower middle income, and 38% from low income (Ibid.: 2). The parents of the children in the wealthiest group, 18%, may be willing to spend significant sums on education. This figure is a basis for business. The 25% upper middle income class may also willing to spend more money for the education of their own children in order to build social mobility. The IFC report recommends private education investment and shows that the market for private education is over USD 400 billion (Ibid.: 3). In the 1960s and 1970s, there was a global trend of societies building solidarity. Welfare spending and national education systems were aspects of this. Since the 1980s, with rising inequality, the wealthiest have arguably lost an interest in solidarity for securing their interests. Rather, they choose to find ways to go around national systems, whether it be for education or healthcare or financial security.

Fourth, since many investors say that they have an interest in education because they wish to make a valuable contribution, institutional investors may be especially supportive. The IFC claims that education investors, including banks and private equity firms, have a secondary objective of providing high-quality education. This objective can make investors less sensitive to bumps in firm performance. This feature makes the sector more protected than other popular investment sectors, such as technology and healthcare (Ibid.: 7–8).

A final factor behind education investment, a factor which deserves extra attention, is that the state offers a layer of protection. There are a few mechanisms behind this protection. While there are investment risks in education, as in any business, it is also an area where the state is willing to step in and prevent firm failure. The state does not want to see children's education jeopardized because of the financial difficulties of a school operator. Private operators of ordinary schools in the United Kingdom, United States, or Sweden sometimes find themselves struggling to keep a given school in the black. Due to insufficient numbers of students or high operating costs, they may be tempted to close the school. Closing branches is, of course, a common practice in many businesses. But in education, it means leaving children without a school to attend. In order to avoid this situation, the state can step into preventing an investment from going bad.

The legal status of many private schools is another form of state-sponsored protection. International schools are frequently registered as charities, even though they are components of wider for-profit entities. This status gives them tax benefits. For example, in Malaysia the operators of international school chains run schools through nonprofit foundations. Even though the parent company is a for-profit enterprise, in, say, property development, the schools are formally parts of a philanthropic foundation. In Hong Kong, with its freer media, criticism appears in the press of the status of Nord Anglia's school there. The headquarters of Nord Anglia Education are in Hong Kong. Nord Anglia's school in the territory is registered as a charity—despite the fact that the parent company is listed on the New York Stock Exchange. As a charity, Nord Anglia's Hong Kong school receives tax exemptions and preferential access to one of the territory's most exclusive assets—land. The high-end Nord Anglia International School reportedly paid only HK $1000, or under US $200, for its prime property. In a city where residents are squeezed into some of the world's densest housing, a land subsidy for an extravagant school, run by a for-profit enterprise, for the wealthiest residents is understandably controversial (Zhao & Tam, 2014).

Because education is easily presented as a public service, these strategies are available for gaining state support. Transnational education corporations (TECs) can

70   6 The Business of International Education

claim to serve the public good while pursuing their corporate interests. The protection helps to make education, including international education, attractive for investment.

Owners of International Schools and Their Interests

A diverse array of interests has become owners of international school groups. A minority are education enterprises controlled by an individual or small group. GEMS, a family-owned firm, is the prime example. Others are firms specializing in other areas, especially property development, who have expanded into international education. Another set, the largest, are owned in whole or part by private equity firms that have moved into education.

From Private Equity to International Education

Institutional investors, either on their own or in collaboration with educators, have been at the forefront of the transformation of international schools into financial assets. Harvey (2005) describes financialization as a fundamental feature of today's world economy. A financialized economy is one in which business activities are oriented to financial returns. Until the 1980s or so, the economy remained production-oriented. Managers sought to maximize output given their resources. A manufacturer of lightbulbs focuses on producing more, higher quality lightbulbs at a lower price. In that model, profit is the goal. In a financialized economy, financial return rather than profit is the aim. Instead of profit from making lightbulbs, the goal is to expand the financial situation of the firm. This may mean securing better returns on property owned, but the main meaning is an orientation to shareholders.

Financialization came about through a transformation in the world economy, according to Harvey. A principal change was a shift to combine managerial and ownership functions in firm leadership. As managers were offered stock options and stock-linked performance rewards, their interests became tied not to production and profit but to the financial health of the firm. Financialization brings with it regular changes, making firms less concerned for their workers (since what they produce is more distantly related to firm aims) and making the economy more like gambling.

In international education, financialization has occurred in distinct ways. The simplest mode of financialization is listing on a stock exchange. Nord Anglia listed on the New York Stock Exchange in 2014. Nord Anglia managers must thus always have one eye on day-to-day fluctuations in stock price. This shifting emphasis is reflected in news about Nord Anglia. A news search on the firm produces as many reports on the stock prices as on its schools. What are the managerial priorities? The stock price or the education business?

Privately-held firms, such as GEMS, are subject less to financialization. Between listing on a stock exchange and being privately held lie most TECs. These are held by consortia of institutional investors. Private equity firms either directly own schools, or are partners in ownership. One example is Sweden's Kunskapsskolan. In order to expand, Kunskapsskolan sold its shares to US private equity firms. Cognita also started with a private equity firm. Even sovereign wealth funds or pension schemes in other countries invest in international schools. The Canadian Teachers' Pension Scheme acquired Busy Bees from Knowledge Universe in 2013. Busy Bees were the UK's largest nursery group and, after its acquisition, it promptly expanded its nurseries in Asia and Canada with the official slogan, as "a global early education organization" (Busy Bees website, http://www.busybeesasia.com/). With a private equity firm, Baring Private Equity Asia Ltd., the Canadian pension scheme also bought a major stake in Nord Anglia in 2017 (Scott, 2017).

From Other Types of Education to International Schools

Some firms in international schools come from other areas of education. Higher education, for example, is a field from which firms can move into international schools. Taylor's Education Group in Malaysia demonstrates this shift. Taylor's holds ten educational institutions, spanning a range of types of schools in including a university. The firm subsequently acquired international schools. The firm kept a lookout for international schools with strong reputations in Malaysia. Its targets included the Garden International School and the Australian International School Malaysia, both schools with long histories and which had been established by expatriate communities. When these schools began to expand, Taylor's came in and purchased them. The local reputation of each school helped Taylor's, which in turn offered stronger financial backing to the schools. Taylor's also assembled a mini-chain of schools under the name Nexus, which has come to include the Nexus International School in Singapore. This approach helped Taylor's become one of the largest K-12 education corporations in Malaysia. Looking beyond its home country, the education conglomerate now plans to make one international school every year overseas.

From Property Development to International Schools, and Vice Versa

Education can be a logical choice of investment for firms in other areas. Property developers do not hold any expertise in education, but in several Asian contexts, it makes sense for a developer to shift into schools. Where high-end developments are newly constructed in expanding urban areas, there is ready-made demand for private schooling. If these developments are sufficiently large and exclusive, having a new international school just outside the gates of the community can make sense. While TECs might step into do this, property firms also expand into international education.

They know it is a lucrative extension of their businesses. As developers, these firms have also solved one of the toughest tasks in establishing a school: acquiring land. An education firm seeking to expand may devote a significant portion of its energy to gaining access to land that is zoned appropriately and in an attractive location. Property firms, who specialize in this task, have an advantage here.

Malaysia is rife with examples of linkages between property development and international education. In some cases, developers and school firms open a partnership. In others, education firms move into real estate, or the other way around. The relationships between property development and schools can become complicated, as the two businesses mix. The British Council, for instance, partnered with YTL Land & Development Berhad in order to establish an international school (British Council, 2015). In another case, Singapore-based Raffles Education in 2015 started a property department, then went on to found the Raffles American School in Johor, Malaysia. A third example is a deal between Alpha Real Estate Investment Trust (REIT) and education firm Paramount, which operates Sri KDU Campus and SRI KDU International School. In August 2017, REIT acquired Paramount. Similar arrangements can be found elsewhere in the region (Tay & Jaafar, 2017). An independent school in the UK, Brighton College, partnered with a real estate firm in order to establish several international schools abroad. Targeting "emerging markets," Brighton set up Brighton International School LTD and opened sister schools in Abu Dhabi, Bangkok, and Dubai (*Edarabia*, 2010; Brighton College International School website, http://www.brightoncollegeinternational.com/About-BCIS-Our-Schools).

International schools have in places become integrated into "gated communities" that have emerged in the suburbs of Malaysian cities. These communities, established and managed by developers, offer all sorts of services to their residents. An upscale development might include a golf course, a park, swimming pools, restaurants, even medical facilities—and, increasingly, an international school. These developments are seen especially outside the capital city, Kuala Lumpur, and in the Nusajaya area across from Singapore. The Sunway example below illustrates this pattern.

An intriguing related example is Mahota, though it is not exactly from the property sector. The family behind the firm operated pig farms in Singapore. When the government decided to close all pork production in Singapore, the family shifted into the supermarket industry. After starting the Prime supermarket chain, the firm expanded into China. In Shanghai, it established a golf course and then founded the Shanghai-Singapore International School. The owners then returned to farming, this time setting up farms in China. It developed an organic farm and a timeshare retreat in rural Shandong. Now, in a few cities, it holds lifestyle spaces with restaurants, organic food shops, art spaces, and natural medicine vendors. These sites are also used to advertise their timeshare in China. In 2016, Mahota opened a kindergarten in Singapore. Mahota offers a range of products that all cater to certain "lifestyle" interests, and international schools fit among them.

Sunway: A Property Firm Enters Education

Sunway University, originally Sunway College, was the first university in Malaysia to make twinning arrangements with foreign universities a principle strategy. In this scheme, students can enroll in the local branch and receive the same degree as if they have studied at the main campus overseas. Founder Jeffrey Cheah established Sunway Group in 1974 as property developer and manager of infrastructure facilities. Then it moved into education. In 1987, Sunway College began working with overseas universities in order, in effect, to import foreign degree-granting capacities. For example, Monash University, in Australia, and Sunway Group Malaysia established Monash University Sunway Campus Malaysia Sdn Bhd (MUSCM). The school was a success in terms of gaining reputation. Many young people who were concerned about their future careers enrolled in the university (Welch, 2011: 73–77). At that time, Sunway Group Malaysia, already expert in facilities management, was well-placed to oversee the physical premises. In this example of Malaysian education internationalization, the overseas partner provided the degree-granting capacity and English-competence training, while the local firm used its know-how in property and facilities.

The difficulties ethnic Chinese face in entering Malaysian universities also made ventures like Sunway's more attracting. For those who could afford the fees, private options like Sunway offered a way around *bumiputra* preference policies. This approach has trickled into primary and secondary schooling as well.

Sunway Group expanded. Sunway College become Sunway University, and then Sunway International School opened. The international school is located in its own development, an exclusive residential property in Johor that is part of a larger Sunway Iskandar development including a hospital, shopping malls, and theme parks. An admission director at the school pointed to the landscape, cluttered with construction machinery as luxury homes were being built around a park-like green space. Parents can live pleasantly in the condominium and make use of the golf course. She added that I should check Sunway's website to see gain a full appreciation for how large the company's international school in Kuala Lumpur is and how well the firm has done. She also emphasized that Sunway operates Malaysia's largest theme park, Sunway Lagoon (fieldwork, August 22, 2017).

From International Schools to Other Businesses

Once an individual or firm owns an international school, there can be opportunities to move into related businesses. Schools need buses, catering services, waste disposal,

74 6 The Business of International Education

and other services. International school chains have reasons, where they are large enough, to expand into these services. GEMS is an example. Given the large number of schools it has, especially in the Middle East, it has opportunities to provide services to itself. Its transportation company owns school buses and provides bus service. Its software arm manages the school network. Through this logic, international education firms can expand to do more than education, their core mission.

How Do International Education Businesses Grow?

I have described how firms can expand into schools from other sectors, and move from schools to supplying related services. But how do school chains grow in the international school space itself?

Sources of Expansion

The creation of education as a business in particular places outside of Asia has contributed to the expansion of international education in Asia. As we saw in Chap. 3, internal economic and political logics in the United Kingdom, the country of origin of some of the largest TECs, drive outward expansion. Since education has become a business in the UK, it could simply expand overseas. More specifically, given that foreign students attend UK schools in such large numbers, British schools could instead go out and set up campuses abroad. The establishment of private schools overseas as well as the creation, at the university level, of overseas campuses, is an extension of—and possibly a substitute for—the business of admitting students from overseas. Traditional British independent schools have launched sister schools abroad in order to boost their revenue, as "overseas expansion could prove a lucrative market for the UK's independent schools" (*EducationInvestor*, April 9, 2009). Business interests in the UK realized that education could be developed as an export industry. Brighton College, Wellington College, Harrow College, Dulwich College, and Oxford High are examples of independent schools that have pursued this strategy. *Education Investor* magazine notes that fifty percent of independent schools aimed to increase their international markets for this purpose. The magazine observes "a hugely aggressive expansion policy" among these schools to establish satellite schools for generate income (Ibid.). Like independent schools, education firms with British origins, such as Cognita and Nord Anglia, rushed to expand through acquisition and building in Asia rather than focusing on the local, British market.

This pattern appears as a "conquest" by Western firms of schooling in Asia. Profits earned abroad have in some cases been funneled back into UK schools. Anthony Seldon, the headmaster of Wellington College and the main force behind the group's overseas expansion, admitted that the profits from Wellington College's satellite campuses will return to the original schools in the UK as bursaries for UK-based students (*EducationInvestor*, Wellington's conquest, Oct. 21, 2010). Seldon explains that Wellington follows the example of a fast food franchise, with consistent logos and menus worldwide, by designing the physical campuses in China and India in the same traditional way as the original school. They sell access to a Western cultural good and status using this modern marketing technique (Ibid.).

Another, more recent reason relates to the UK's departure from the European Union. Brexit is expected to make it more difficult for international students to enter the UK. In response, schools will likely expand their overseas operations to find students. UK firms particularly focus on going out and building their own schools since these international students might not be able to come to the UK easily anymore (*Education Investor* Transnational education—a global race? February 27, 2017). Many go to the UK for study, the largest number from China, Hong Kong, and Russia. Other countries will step in once entry to the UK becomes more difficult. France is excited to embrace more international students after Brexit (*Education Investor*, The Macron effect, Sept. 2017, 34–35). This reason further encourages UK private schools and education corporations to set up satellite campuses (regional branches) in the Asia-Pacific in particular. According to Research group HEGlobal, since 2012, international students in the UK declined while the overseas activities of UK-based transnational education institutions expanded (*EducationInvestor*, June 29, 2016). Further, there are already more than 100 international university partnerships that deliver degrees following Western standards (*EducationInvestor*, Nov. 3, 2015).

Building Brands?

A current question for TECs is whether to build their chains as brands or rely on the reputation of individual schools within those chains. There can be a strong temptation to build a brand and use the brand as a main means of marketing. Such a move is also in keeping with the emergence of international education as a consumer good. On the other hand, most schools under TECs are ones that have been acquired rather than newly built. These schools have local reputations and branding the schools may be of little help.

Branded school chains have appeared in other parts of the global education industry. Srivastava argues that school chains, for example Bridge International Academies (BIA), consider themselves to be the "Starbucks" of schools as they can open low-fee private schools implement standardized management and curricula (Srivastava, 2016). This tendency can now be seen in schools ranging from inexpensive private schools targeting poorer groups to elite international schools.

The various options in relation to branding can be seen in the biggest TECs. The Global Indian International School (GIIS), for example, runs schools throughout Asia that follow a single model and use the GIIS label. The group even made its teaching methodology (called "Nine Gems") proprietary. All GIIS branches employ this methodology. Another nonprofit chain, the Delhi Public School also operates under a single name in different jurisdictions. Among for-profit school groups, GEMS

Education has the most experience in trying to build a single, global brand in the international school sector. Most GEMS schools keep the GEMS name. The logo is prominently displayed at the schools and in brochures. Admissions officers and promotional materials for any one school place the GEMS reputation at the center of advertising efforts. With schools at different price levels, GEMS has sought to sell products aimed at consumers of different income levels while developing a single, global brand.

Even as elite education becomes a global consumer item, developing schools into a brand faces special challenges. Paying tuition for a school is not exactly the same as buying a handbag or a cup of coffee. Parents need only choose once or a few times while their children are school age. Consumption decisions are not continually made. For education firms, operating a school is also not the same as running a retail outlet. The costs to open (or acquire) a school are enormous, upwards of USD 100 million.[1] When establishing a school, this cost includes the work that needs to be done finding and acquiring a desirable piece of land that is zoned properly for a school. Each new branch also requires educating "consumers" on the brand.

When a firm has investors who demand quick returns, the challenge to building a brand becomes even greater. Private equity groups appreciate the stability of education as a sector and they aim for relatively fast returns on their investments, with profits arriving in three to five years. As an executive at the consulting firm Gabbitas says of for-profit school groups, "unfortunately, too many of these ventures fall foul of the need to satisfy ever-thirsty private equity investors who wish to see more immediate returns than even the most successful school can deliver without compromising on its educational philosophy and culture" (Wylie, 2012). Several TECs, therefore, give up on trying to establish brands or even on building new schools. Returns can be quicker if the firms acquires a school and continues to run it under the old name. Cognita pursues this strategy. Singapore's Stamford American International School is the only school the firm has built anywhere, despite the firm being one of the biggest international school chains. None of its Asian schools have "Cognita" in the name.

Nord Anglia also does more acquiring than establishing, though it does run several schools under the Nord Anglia name. The firm has a new, flagship school at its Hong Kong headquarters and it is named the Nord Anglia International School. While the company prefers to stay behind the scenes, it also places indicators that a school belongs to them. On school gates, "A Nord Anglia school" may be written. All schools in the group have a website with Nord Anglia domain.

There is also a pattern of brands within brands. In this pattern, transnational organizations allow schools under them to remain associated with a smaller chain or with a national education system. Taylor's Education Group operates schools directly under its name and separately under the Nexus brand. In its promotional material Cognita highlights the advantages of a school that belongs to an international network, but it also develops school-specific identities and retains pre-existing brand names.

---

[1] Newly-established schools in the higher price range cost USD 200–300 million to start, depending on the location. A valuation of Nord Anglia Education in 2017 put its schools at an average value of USD 100 million per school (Deveau 2017).

The Stamford American International School obviously draws on the value of an "American" education, while the Singapore Australian International School appeals to those who think highly of Australia's education system. Cognita and Nord Anglia have even split previously existing clusters of schools. The two firms have purchased portions of the Saint Andrews group of international schools in Thailand—even as that name persists, one of the schools is run by Nord Anglia while three are operated by Cognita. There are also distinct labels under brands. When Taylor's Education acquired an international school in Singapore, it was rebranded as Nexus International School rather than Taylor's—even though many of its education operations are named after the company.

Among the large TECs, GEMS is the most financially independent. It is not a publicly listed company nor is it run by a private equity firm (though GEMS boss Sunny Varkey sold off a piece of the company to a private equity firm before retaking it). The Varkeys say that GEMS is a "family business," a theme Dino Varkey, executive director at GEMS and Sunny Varkey's son, proudly stressed at a public event at the GEMS World Academy (GWA) Singapore in January 2015. The Varkeys raise their own capital and therefore can experiment more with the business. It is little surprise, then, that GEMS has built more of its own schools than other TECs have, and, more than any other firm, GEMS has attempted to create a global brand especially through GWA schools. Dino Varkey points out that "capital and infrastructure funds have a three- to five-year investment horizon. They don't understand that education has a seven-year gestation, and the first dollar of profit could only come in year eight" (Rai, 2014). With more autonomy, it is easier for GEMS to mobilize a few hundred million dollars in capital on a single, long-term project than it would be for public corporations or private equity firms.

The corporatization of international schools has thus produced tendencies in two distinct directions. One tendency, driven by goals of earning short-term revenues, is toward decentralized management of international school chains. The other tendency, when organizations are more ambitious, is toward the creation of chains of international schools under a single, valued brand. In both scenarios school management becomes a global operation. The latter tendency leads to the construction of an education product that is the same in different places in content and value. Where this element is stronger, organizations are attempting to sell a single product on a global scale. Acquisitions- and management-oriented firms like Cognita do not sell a single product worldwide. It is too early to conclude that a consumer brand-like notion of global underpins international schools. However, we can see that a few large organizations are attempting to move in this direction. The practical changes that have made these efforts possible relate to the worldwide reach of several education organizations.

Trends in preschools, or "early education," may foreshadow what could happen in international education. The past several years have seen rapid turnover in ownership of early education centers in Asia. Chains have emerged in particular cities, then those have been acquired by larger firms. Complicated trades and mergers have occurred, as the Busy Bees example illustrates. Franchising has also emerged as an important means of expanding brands. For example, Eton House began as a small preschool in

Singapore and now has become a transnational education group, advising on early education for the Singapore and Chinese governments and expanding its international school business beyond early education in several countries including South Korea, China and Malaysia. Operators apply for Eton House branding and then run the schools independent of Eton House, just as a convenience store boss pays for rights to the name. Franchising has not yet appeared as a major strategy in international schools. Given the example of preschools, it would not be surprising if the strategy became more widely adopted. On the other hand, the startup costs for a preschool are much lower, in part because they tend to be smaller in scale, than international schools. This factor may make franchising more appropriate for preschools.

In light of these considerations, decisions on branding seem driven by the ownership structures of the firms. A publicly-listed firm may not have the time horizon to invest in building multiple schools around the world. Acquiring new firms can require as much capital but it can also produce results immediately. The pressures may be similar for firms owned mostly by private equity firms. It is simpler to buy schools that have an existing reputation. Mostly privately-owned firms have tended toward branding, because they can plan longer for the future.

How Do TECs Find Customers?

International schools tend to cluster in places. Parents then have decisions to make over which school is most appropriate for their children. In this market, parents have to see what is available and collect information that will help them make a decision. For schools, it means marketing is one of their major activities. Schools hold information sessions for prospective parents, admissions officers take families on tours, and marketing teams put out advertisements. One of the main strategies of international schools is to demonstrate that they are prestigious.

Demonstrating Prestige

The challenges to demonstrating prestige are not the same for all schools. Some schools begin with a prestigious name, and there is little challenge at all. The clearest examples are old British independent schools that have sought to tap into their name value to earn extra revenue by setting up campuses in Asia (Bunnell, 2009). Possessing a valued name, the opportunity to establish an international school is almost too good to pass up. The situation is different for a firm like UAE-based GEMS, especially when it operates in East or Southeast Asia. While GEMS has a reputation as a school operator in the Gulf states, most parents elsewhere would be unfamiliar with the name. Lacking pedigree, GEMS has to demonstrate that its school is a prestigious one. It is little surprise, then, that GEMS issues a brochure entitled "University destinations: where our students go," which is decorated with the logos of Stanford, Harvard, Cambridge, and other famous universities.

GEMS also distributes brochures featuring major world figures like corporate leaders, astronauts, and even former heads of government. Bill Clinton and Tony Blair have arrangements with GEMS, and they have given special lectures for GEMS. Sending your children to a GEMS school can give the impression that you join an elite circle of global movers and shakers.

Another way to demonstrate prestige is to charge high fees. The chain Avenues offers an example of this approach. The firm sets school fees at a very high level, seeming to indicate the quality and exclusivity of the education. Whether this strategy is successful may depend on context. In China, for example, families have turned away from many of the most expensive foreign-affiliated international schools, as domestic chains offer a similar experience at a fraction of the cost. GEMS is just as blunt in its pricing strategy. Owner Sunny Varkey is fond of comparing his firm to an airlines business. Just as an airline offers economy, business, and first class tickets, GEMS offers schools at Tier 1 to Tier 4 levels. Varkey explained the logic with brutal clarity: "We adopted the airline model of economy, business and first class to make top-notch education available based on what families could afford" (Rai, 2014). In Dubai and India GEMS has several "economy" schools. Many of the premium international schools around the world fall under its Gems World Academy and GEMS Modern Academy labels. As with airfare, the prices vary dramatically with class. Annual tuition ranges between USD 300 and USD 40,000 across the four tiers. Schools can also boast about the high salaries given to staff. An admissions officer I spoke with emphasized that: "We pay the highest salary to teaching assistants. And our school pays one of the highest salaries to teachers here" (fieldwork 2014). The insinuation is that price stands in for quality.

Investment in facilities is a common way for international schools to attract customers. Schools routinely place their facilities at the forefront of their promotional efforts. Many of these facilities are state-of-the-art, often well beyond what most students could benefit from. How does an Olympic-sized swimming pool help a primary-school student? What value is there in having a Michelin-starred chef running the cafeteria? Does a school need to have its own planetarium? Despite facilities seeming a poor fit with the needs of children, school operators spend heavily on facilities and stress them when advertising. It may be that education is a difficult thing to describe in a short sales pitch. Facilities can be seen directly by families of prospective students, and that may make them more compelling on sales grounds.

Similar to investment in facilities, investment in technology is a visible, tangible way to communicate prestige. Many schools run by TECs bring a good deal of technology into the classroom. Smartboards—whiteboards equipped with computers—are common. Students are usually given their own tablets. One school even distributed tablets to five-year-old preschool children, who are supposed to submitted electronic portfolios weekly. Teachers could then evaluate their work.

Schools also demonstrate prestige by showcasing their connections to those who already are prestigious. A visit to a newly-established international school in Singapore, run by an TEC, made this approach clear. "Our technology advisor worked for

Steve Jobs at Apple," an admissions officer, dressed for the corporate world, told me. She continued, "even the head of the IB office joined us." She emphasized that IB staff send their children to the school. "The IB people are our friends." The swimming coach had previously trained the national team; the chef was from a five-star hotel; the music teacher had a Juliard degree. These references are the everyday stuff of marketing for an international school run by an TEC.[2]

IB and the "Economization" of Education

No discussion of international school marketing could leave out consideration of curricula such as IB or IGCSE. IB has gained increasing prominence in academic treatment of international schools (Ledger, 2017). Moreover, mention of these is ubiquitous in promotional material for international schools. Of course, the purpose of these programs has little to do with marketing. Rather, they are approaches to providing education. The IB philosophy, for example, stresses "holistic education" with a stress on aspects of growth that cannot or should not be evaluated in some linear manner. The walls of an IB classroom are typically decorated with slogans about "kindness" or "thoughtfulness." Especially in Asian contexts, these messages are completely different from ideas of standardized, hierarchical, test-based learning. For parents wishing to try a new, friendlier teaching method, the IB program appeals. And, for sure, there are many teachers who excel at tapping into this philosophy to educate their pupils.

IB, though, takes on other meanings outside the classroom. IB has become a signal of quality, a brand in itself. Parents—in my experience—often struggle to understand IB, but the fact that a school is marked as IB approved sends a message to parents. Organizations like IB, or Cambridge's International General Certificate of Secondary Education (IGCSE), or the International Primary Curriculum (IPC) are crucial partners for TECs. In 2016, it was estimated that half of the world's 8000 international schools offer IB (SIIA, 2016). Since independent schools worldwide take up these curricula, they are widely known to parents and to admissions officers at leading universities. By linking their school brands to these curriculum and diploma brands, TECs have an easier time selling their schools (Gardner-McTaggart, 2016; Lee & Wright, 2016; Wright, Lee, Tang, & Tsui, 2016). References to these programs allow parents of potential students to process a great deal of information. One need not simply trust the Nord Anglia brand; through trust in IB or Cambridge one can trust a Nord Anglia school. The TECs enthusiastically hitch their reputations to these programs, which are already better known. Without these partners, school groups would have far greater difficulty explaining what they have to offer. In Asia, the prestige attached to IB is recent. For the first four decades of IB's existence, it did not have this reputation. In the past ten years, it has become big. Parents are familiar with the name, and schools splash it across their marketing activities.

---

[2]Fieldwork conducted on Dec. 1, 2014 at an international school in Singapore.

An advertisement for the Nexus International School painted on a two-story bus in Singapore included words of praise from IB.

If schools have found IB useful for business activities, the International Baccalaureate Organization (IBO) has also moved in a more corporate direction. IBO, based in Switzerland, is officially a nonprofit organization.[3] It is also a major global organization with substantial annual revenue. Thousands of schools worldwide, include 314 in East and Southeast Asia, use the IB curriculum (calculated from www.ibo.org). A main source of revenue is the charging of fees to schools that adopt the IB program. In 2013 it earned USD 162 million in revenue from school fees (IBO website, https://www.ibo.org/. Accessed February 2014). Schools that wish to gain IB accreditation must pay a fee to IBO, which then conducts a series of inspections of the school before giving it the right to offer an official IB diploma. Schools using the IB curriculum continue to pay fees to IBO for the regular inspection and IBO exams. Since revenue is generated from registering schools, IBO has a stake in expanding its curriculum to more and more schools. It is therefore understandable that marketing and expansion are priorities for IBO.

These trends have placed the pedagogical content of IB at odds with IB's business function. The slogan of "holistic education" has in some ways overwhelmed the original meaning of "holistic education." Schools, parents, and IBO itself have given the slogan more attention than they have given the content. This shift relates to education's "economization." Schools have become oriented to another output, in this case to producing students who can ascend a global education hierarchy. Standardized labels, like IB or IGCSE, fit nicely with a context in which parents consume education. All the incentives of a market run against the thoughtful consideration required to reflect on whether one wishes an IB experience for one's child. The label is much easier.

A clear example of IB's economization is the emergence—in Singapore and presumably elsewhere—of private tutoring services for preparing for IB examinations. Students completing an IB diploma are required to sit for, and pass, a set of exams in their final year. These exams are graded, but as long as a minimum score is reached, students receive the diploma. Moreover, the philosophy of IB opposes extra study outside of the curriculum. Programs are tailored to individuals, who should not be judged in a standard way. In Asia, where public school systems are accompanied by private tuition centers, an IB education is a chance to avoid the stress of the private tuition childhood. Nonetheless, being nested within a corporatized education environment has built competitive pressures on IB exams. In Singapore, tuition centers, or "cram schools," dedicated to IB exam preparation have become popular among families with children in IB programs (Ong, 2016). Even though the IB philosophy opposes the style of cram schools, that style dovetails with IB education in certain contexts. This example shows how the social meaning of schools can undermine the promised distinctive IB education.

---

[3]IGCSE is also nonprofit. IPC is for-profit.

Who Runs Schools?

Who are the people operating and working for international schools run by TECs? Considering the staff can reveal insight into how these firms work.

Circulation of Teachers

Working as a teacher in an international school can be one of the most rewarding and meaningful jobs. An amazing corps of people have spent their careers travelling around the world, moving every three or five years, gaining a cosmopolitan sensibility, imparting knowledge to others. Such work could seem disruptive and unstable to many others. With the expansion of TECs, the profession of teaching in international schools has changed.

Retaining staff can be a tremendous challenge, and it is a challenge that reveals a lesson about international schools. In the school where I worked, teachers would regularly move to another school for a slight pay increase. School administrators could become frustrated by such moves, as they are disruptive to HR departments and to teaching plans. These moves can become a source of tension in international schools. But there is no reason to blame teachers, as they merely act to protect their interests in the job market. What is important to see is the reason why teachers are able to shift. If corporatization led international schools to distinguish themselves from each other in terms of the education they deliver, then we would expect schools to develop unique curricula with their own pedagogies. Schools would then need to devote substantial resources to training and retaining teachers. Yet teachers appear to be interchangeable. What staff rotation indicates is that expectations for teaching in different international schools have converged. A teacher can move seamlessly from one to the next because the ways they teach are so similar. Most teach in English. As international schools are now tied less to different foreign school systems, teachers can be mobile. Familiarity with the IB or IGCSE programs can make it easier for a teacher to move to another IB or IGCSE school. In particular, if you have taught in an IB school, then you can be called an IB teacher. This is a norm—even though there is officially no such category as an "IB teacher." International school teachers often aspire to be at an IB school so they can gain this informal credential, thereby increasing their market value. A Canadian teacher who shifted from one international school to another, which was applying for IB accreditation, was disappointed to learn that there was no special IB training (fieldwork 2012).

Under these circumstances, a favored way to find teachers is to poach them from other schools. When a new school opens in town, or expands, it will inevitably look to rival schools for teachers. Schools may also turn to the international labor market for teachers in international schools. Large international fairs for teachers are held regularly. These events are opportunities for aspiring teachers to match themselves with international schools. None of these points is to say that teacher quality in corporate international schools is poor. The teachers may be very good. However, the business of international education contributes to an approach that makes each school less distinctive. The rotation of teachers is evidence of that effect.

School Management

The managers of international schools sit between the offices of TECs and the teachers. Managers include school principals, (or heads of school) deputy principals, admissions officers, and marketing specialists, among others. School heads often come from the ranks of teaching staff. After building careers teaching in international schools, their seniority makes them candidates for management positions. The dramatic change in their fortunes needs to be appreciated. After working as teachers in various schools, they suddenly find themselves reporting to the corporate headquarters of a major business. They could not have anticipated this situation. Now, they work as representatives not of a school but of a corporation.

Other officers may come from different backgrounds. The first point of contact at a school for the parents of prospective students is the admissions director. Those in charge of admissions and marketing are unlikely to have any background in education. Rather, they are recruited from various sectors of the corporate world. Knowledge specific to schools may not be a requirement for the positions. Experience with sales, even if in an unrelated sector, may be deemed more important. Selling a school may be more like selling something else than it is like performing another role in a school.

The diversity of home countries—not to mention host countries—is rarely reflected in the staff of international schools. In English-language schools, white faces dominate. They speak with a range of accents. British teachers are common. Many are social climbers who were intrepid enough to leave home and seek prosperity or adventure abroad. "Global" is one word to describe the administration of international schools. Another would be "colonial." Especially to an Asian clientele, perhaps, whiteness plays a role in sending a signal to parents about the status of a school (Gardner-McTaggart 2018). The point here is that the staff of international schools do not represent some culturally neutral global elite; race and English-language fluency are important markers that may signal status hierarchies to Asian parents.

Conclusion

A consultant for international schools in China touts her expertise in two fields: international education and luxury brands. She expects that the growth of international schools will be fast for local students in Hong Kong and China. Chinese parents' desire to send their children overseas for university encourages the expansion of international schools. She points out that "just like their obsession with luxury goods, it seems that Chinese also have an obsession with brand-name universities" (Ge, 2015). What do international schools have in common with luxury brands? That these specializations can come together encapsulates the transformation that has occurred with corporatization of international schools. "International education" is less about "education" (as in, teaching students) than it is a business activity that happens to involve schools. Fifteen years ago this was not the case. Educating children is incidental to the core operations of an international school chain. The focus is not on providing a community service but on ensuring the financial health of the organization. Education has become a side activity for property developers rather than the domain of educationists. Schools invest in over-the-top facilities and in demonstrating prestige rather than seeking to differentiate the substance of the educational experiences they offer.

Compared with corporatization in educational systems or the appearance of private-public school partnerships in development assistance work, this transformation in international schools has received less attention. There would appear to be good reason. International schools account for a relatively small proportion of students anywhere, and what happens in this sphere does not directly impinge on school systems. For this reason, international schools can be presented more as a "private" matter than a public one. The children and families involved are also not vulnerable. Even if firms take advantage of students and their families, such as by raising fees regularly, the outcry is muted because these are the privileged in society.

But the main reason to be interested in international schools has little to do with families whose children attend them. A particular political effect has followed the corporatization of international education. Because institutional investors, managing pensions and savings for people across the world, put money into international education, many of us are now tied to this business. If our money is in this "sector," then our interest is in the business of education. Our savings are tied to the business success of education firms. Financial news on schools now accounts for a big portion of public information on international education. But what are the collective consequences of these firms' financial success? Growth in these firms can have consequences well beyond international education. As we have seen, many simultaneously hold interests in fields outside of international schools. Just as international school groups have become an issue for public concern, we have been tied to them in ways that point us away from critical scrutiny.

There are indications that TECs have growing public influence. They articulate visions for what education should be. They have collaborations and partnerships with major international institutions. Influential individuals lend support to them, and governments hire them for advice. TECs have ambitions on a global scale. This scale is the subject I turn to next.

References

Baltodano, M. (2012). Neoliberalism and the demise of public education: the corporatization of schools of education. *International Journal of Qualitative Studies in Education, 25*(4): 487–507.

Brighton College International Schools website. http://www.brightoncollegeinternational.com/About-BCIS-Our-Schools. Accessed August 10, 2018.

British Council. (2015). *New British Council school in Malaysia announced.* https://www.britishcouncil.org/organisation/press/new-british-council-school-malaysia-announced. Accessed July 23, 2018.

Bunnell, T. (2009). The exporting and franchising of elite English private schools: The emerging 'second wave'. *Asia Pacific Journal of Education, 28*(4), 383–393.

Busy Bees website. http://www.busybeesasia.com/. Accessed January 2018.

Deveau, S. (2017. April 25). Canadian pension group to buy Nord Anglia at $4.3 billion value. *Bloomberg.* https://www.bloomberg.com/news/articles/2017-04-25/canadian-pension-board-group-to-buy-nord-anglia-for-4-3-billion. Accessed July 11, 2018.

Eduarabia. (September 2010). Bloom properties to commence construction of Brighton College school in Abu Dhabi. https://www.edarabia.com/8616/bloom-properties-to-commence-construction-of-brighton-college-school-in-abu-dhabi/. Accessed August 10, 2018.

EducationInvestor, April 9, 2009.

EducationInvestor. (2010, October 21)Wellington's conquest.

EducationInvestor, November 3, 2015.

EducationInvestor, June 29, 2016.

EducationInvestor. (2017, February 27). Transnational education—A global race?.

EducationInvestor. (September 2017). The Macron effect (pp. 34–35).

Gardner-McTaggart, A. (2016). International elite, or global citizens? Equity, distinction and power: The International Baccalaureate and the rise of the South. *Globalisation, Societies and Education, 14*(1), 1–29.

Gardner-McTaggart, A. (2018). The Promise of Advantage: Englishness in IB International Schools. *Perspectives: Policy and Practice in Higher Education, 22*(4): 109–114.

Ge, C. (2015, September 7). China's booming international school business untouched by slowdown. *South China Morning Post.* https://www.scmp.com/business/china-business/article/1855932/chinas-booming-international-school-business-untouched. Accessed August 10, 2018.

Harvey, D. (2005). *A brief history of neoliberalism.* New York: Oxford University Press.

IBO website. https://www.ibo.org/. Accessed February 2014.

IFC. (2010). *Education Investment Guide: A guide for investors in private education in emerging markets.* International Finance Corporation World Bank Group.

Ledger, S. (2017). The International Baccalaureate standards and practices as reflected in literature (2009–2016). *The International Schools Journal, 37*(1), 32–44.

Lee, M., & Wright, E. (2016). Moving from elite international schools to the world's elite universities. *International Journal of Comparative Education and Development, 18*(2), 120–136.

Lubienski, C. (2005). Public schools in marketized environments: Shifting incentives and unintended consequences of competition-based educational reforms. *American Journal of Education, 111*(4), 464–486.

Ong, J. (2016, May 13). Behind Singapore's Success in the IB: More tuition? *Channel News Asia.* https://www.channelnewsasia.com/news/singapore/behind-singapore-s-success-in-the-ib-more-tuition-8000894. Accessed May 10, 2018.

Rai, S. (2014, April 2). Billionaire education entrepreneur Varkey takes his Dubai school chain worldwide. *Forbes.* https://www.forbes.com/sites/saritharai/2014/04/02/chalk-a-block/#56fc3f7e4e75. Accessed July 24, 2018.

Saltman, K. J. (2005). *The Edison schools: Corporate schooling and the assault on public education.* New York: Routledge.

Scott, D. (2017, April 25). Canadian pension group to buy Nord Anglia at $4.3 billion value. *Bloomberg.* https://www.bloomberg.com/news/articles/2017-04-25/canadian-pension-board-group-to-buy-nord-anglia-for-4-3-billion. Accessed July 22, 2018.

SIIA website. (2016, April 19). *Global webinar conference: Going global, international school markets—IB Edition.* https://www.siia.net/Divisions/ETIN-Education-Technology-Industry-Network/Resources/Webinars/Going-Global-International-School-Markets-International-Baccalaureate-Edition. Accessed February 2018.

Srivastava, P. (2016). Questioning the global scaling up of low-fee private schooling: The nexus between business, philanthropy, and PPPs. In A. Verger, C. Lubienski, & G. Steiner-Khamsi (Eds.), *World yearbook of education 2016: The global education indistry* (pp. 248–263). New York: Routledge.

Tay, C., & Jaafar, S.S. (2017). Paramount Corp acquires 66% stake in REAL Education group for RM183 mil. *The Edge Markets.* http://www.theedgemarkets.com/article/paramount-corp-acquires-66-stake-real-education-group-rm183-mil. Accessed August 20, 2018.

Welch, A. (2011). *Higher education in Southeast Asia: Blurring borders, changing balance.* London: Routledge.

Wright, E., Lee, M., Tang, H., & Tsui, G. C. P. (2016). Why offer the International Baccalaureate Middle Years Programme? A comparison between schools in Asia-Pacific and other regions. *Journal of Research in International Education, 15*(1), 3–17.

Wylie, I. (2012, December 13). Education goes global. *Financial Times.* http://www.ft.com/cms/s/0/0e3cdd0e-428f-11e2-95fc-00144feabdc0.html#axzz3Os3nM6RT. Accessed February 1, 2015.

Zhao, S., & Tam, J. (2014, June 3). Tax-free school rules attacked Tax-free status for schools attacked. *South China Morning Post.* https://www.scmp.com/news/hong-kong/article/1524102/tax-free-status-hong-kongs-international-schools-attacked. Accessed July 22, 2018.

Chapter 7
International Education Goes Global: Transnational Education Corporations as Global Actors

"Global" is a word that appears everywhere in connection with the international education business. In promotional material, the larger firms boast of their global operations. They highlight their affiliations with international institutions such as UNICEF or with well-known charities with worldwide reach. "Global" is ubiquitous, too, in descriptions of pedagogy. Schools promise not an international education but a "global" one. A commonly-stated goal is to develop "global citizens" to meet the challenges of the future.

Undoubtedly, "global" is a buzzword of our times. Firms seize on this popular term and try to use it for marketing purposes. We could dismiss this fixation as only so much propaganda, but a more careful reading suggests there is something here. The point is not the word "global" itself. That term could be changed for another such as "cosmopolitan" or "worldwide" or something else; it is just that "global" happens to be popular more generally today. The key point here is the meaning, not the word. Education firms do operate on a global—or worldwide—scale, and they interact with institutions at that level. They also possess an idea of what a cosmopolitan education can be. They have a vision and they work with actors that deal in symbols on a global scale.

There are two issues here that might be taken separately. One has to do with how education firms appeal to parents and how they educate children. These are questions of what "global" means in schools. The other has to do with interactions with international institutions. These two issues should be considered together. Both relate to ways that education firms link to international power. What is their vision of "global" and how do they propagate it? This question is one of ideology and how it relates to the exercise of power. I argue that international school chains advocate a particular notion of global. This chapter teases out that meaning and examines ways that firms perpetuate it.

© The Author(s), under exclusive license to Springer Nature Singapore Pte Ltd.,
part of Springer Nature 2019
H. Kim, *How Global Capital is Remaking International Education*,
SpringerBriefs in Education, https://doi.org/10.1007/978-981-32-9672-5_7

These are questions about how education firms relate to global governance. How does this business relate to the architecture of global power? Before turning to what "global" means, we should explore a concept that has been developed. Education scholars have picked up on the idea of "global policy networks." In this model, policy is not something narrowly made by states or supranational entities. Rather, it is advocated by a mélange of private and public actors, organizations, and individuals, who lend support and money to particular public policy ideas. This concept is useful for grasping the "global" in the international education business.

Global Education Policy Networks

Research on education policy and the global education industry converge on the point that education policy is increasingly a global matter involving many sorts of actors. This set of actors can be viewed either from the context of domestic education policymaking, or of an international education industry. Let us take the former first. Writing on education policy, especially in the British context, Stephen Ball and his colleagues have drawn attention to the influence of education policy networks that have a global reach. While the education ministry still formally governs education, with substantial powers devolved to local governments, the actors who make policy are embedded in other relationships and flows of ideas. For example, privatizing reforms in the 1990s arose not in isolation but in a transnational flow of ideas. Think tanks in the United States and United Kingdom propagated ideas about how and why for-profit schooling would be good. Receptive politicians took on and championed these ideas. School firms also advocated for them. When Sweden embraced such reforms, UK reformers were quick to sponsor their advice. In this way, a group of actors located in different parts of the world, spanning private and public organizations, became policy advocates. These were think tanks, education businesses, government actors, academics. Together they comprise a global education policy network. The model of a network can be more useful for thinking about education policy than a model of regulators and a field. In a globalizing context, it is helpful to think about education policy in network terms (Ball, 2012).

The global education policy network also appears when the focus is on the business of education. In literature on the global education industry, a main point is that private and public actors become intertwined. Recent studies of the global education industry observe that a multitude of actors have become involved in shaping education policy. Advocacy groups and businesses pressure states to adopt certain policies, or exert influence by converting areas of public service into economic sectors. As Gulson and Lubienski (2014) point out, "non-government dimensions are becoming crucial to understanding education policy changes." In this "heterarchical" landscape, governments, communities, international organizations, businesses, and philanthropic endeavors are enmeshed in relationships that influence education (Olmedo, 2014).

Global Education Policy Networks

In these ways, governmental actors become implicated in the business of education, and policymaking is an activity that is influenced from many areas.

Relationships tie together actors in a policy network. Sponsorship is one type of relationship. Think tanks of a particular ideological stripe give grants to support the research of particular academics. Or else, a foundation commissions a report from a scholar. Another relationship is when high-profile individuals lend their public support to a particular cause in education. They are paid for being affiliated or making public appearances. Revolving doors are of course another type of relationship. Regulators move into industry; government hires industry insiders to regulate.

Besides the actors (nodes) and relationships (conduits) of a network, another feature is the set of ideas that are put forward. An effect or activity of a network is to advocate for a set of ideas. While there are different ideas about education policy, much attention is given to neoliberal ideas and their networks. Here a discussion of a prominent education policy network can illustrate how this works.

Privatization of education is an aim of the most prominent global education policy networks. A central idea is that governments cannot "deliver" education as efficiently, to the right people, at a high enough quality, as the private sector can. Competitive market pressures can drive profit-oriented school operators to out-perform public sector counterparts. There are many variations on this logic, which travels to a variety of contexts. In the developing world, for example, it may be emphasized that the state is too corrupt or incompetent to oversee schooling. In a place like the United States, stress might be given to the advantages of "choice" for parents that should appear with the creation of education markets. Academics, inspired by Milton Friedman, the father of neoliberalism, have sketched these ideas out, often with support from conservative think tanks such as the Heritage Foundation.

Major international institutions have picked up on and endorsed variants of this privatizing mantra in education. Joel Spring documents the involvement of these organizations in this project of "education economization," that is, the transformation of education into an activity oriented to serving the economy. The World Bank's main missions are to eliminate poverty and support development in poorer countries. In order to pursue these tasks, the World Bank has developed a strategy on education. This strategy centers on viewing people as human capital and identifying ways that this human capital can be made useful in the economy. Private education providers, in this view, should have clearer ideas about how to transform young people into useful, employable human assets. This perspective has been buttressed by another position embraced and promoted by the World Bank: the simple idea that government roles should give way to private roles in education (Spring, 2015: 82). The economization of education encompasses both turning education into a business and making schools oriented to developing people who are useful to the economy.

A report titled "Learning for All Investing in People's Knowledge and Skills to Promote Development: World Bank Group Education Strategy 2020" yields insight into World Bank thinking on education. The publication emphasizes that degrees are a poor measure of education's contribution to development. The degrees may equip students only with abstract understanding and not with the practical skills that prepare one for work. Instead, the document asserts, education should endow young people with skills for the workplace. Strategy 2020 advocates greater attention to critical thinking, problem solving and team skills, as these will serve graduates and the economy better in the long run (Spring, 2015: 70; World Bank, 2011). This emphasis, incidentally, matches precisely with curricula offered in many international schools.

Similar ideas appear in programs from the World Economic Forum (WEF), which holds its showcase event in Davos annually. The world's largest corporations attend the WEF, and it betrays a corporate approach to education. Take, for example, a statement in a WEF document. The WEF's Education Initiative outlines a plan to "integrate entrepreneurship education into all levels of education" (Spring, 2015: 105). This goal is another version of the economization of education. The emphasis here is not on creating valuable workers but on fostering business-minded people through education. Spring introduces the organization's claim from the website, "Business should be involved in shaping curricula" (Ibid., 106). Some international schools have already begun practicing this advice. One of the most expensive international schools in Singapore, the Stamford American School, boasts an "Innovation Centre" that was praised upon its establishment for serving "as a platform for research projects and partnerships between Stamford's students and business corporations" (*MTI* October 19, 2012). Students learn in ways that may be useful for business.

The WEF also advocates partnerships between governments and business in education. Their actions are not only "involved in shaping curricula," but also seek "to shape global, regional and industry agendas" (cited in Spring, 2015: 106). WEF initiatives such as this one are important in setting agendas that gain attention in the media. This forms another component of the neoliberal global education policy network.

Both the World Bank and the WEF have been crucial in linking the private education sector to national governments to form public-private partnerships (PPPs) (Spring, 2015: 111). The WEF also works with the United Nations Education, Social, and Cultural Organization (UNESCO). In conjunction with the WEF, UNESCO held a meeting on "Partnerships with the Private Sector in Education for All" in 2004. In the decade of the 2000s, PPPs blossomed in education. Encouragement from the global policy network involving WEF, the World Bank, and UN agencies lies behind that trend. Prestigious and influential international actors propagate a certain range of policy ideas in education.

Researchers are important parts of these networks. Robertson and Verger (2012) criticize scholars who collaborate with institutions to promote PPPs in education. These researchers cite each other and strengthen each others' messages repeatedly, while tending to ignore other opinions (Verger, Fontdevila, & Zancajo, 2016: 154–155). Research can be used for the purpose of privatizing education.

Returning to international education, we might expect that transnational education corporations (TECs) operating in this area may have little to do with policy networks. After all, TECs in this space do not seek to reform education systems. Compared to those firms that run schools in the school system, or provide services to those schools, international school firms would seem to depend less on basic education policy. They have found space to operate in the corners and crevices of main education systems. However, as we have seen in Chap. 3, policy remains crucial to international education, in particular policies on how international schools relate to the school system. This is just one way that policy matters for businesses in this field. In fact, TECs are fully immersed in global education policy networks, including in the one described above. GEMS Education, for example, participates actively in the WEF, while Nord Anglia has partnerships with UNICEF. It is therefore worth considering how international education fits into these global policy networks. Before turning to the actors and their relationships, we should figure out what idea they might be advocating.

The Meanings of a "Global" Education

In an interconnected world, the aspiration to educate young people to have a global rather than parochial outlook is a noble ambition. We need people who understand multiple cultures. Especially as the world faces global planetary challenges, which require cooperation across national boundaries, this sensibility is crucial. United World College was founded on this premise decades ago. Today that mission would seem at least as relevant as in the past.

International schools promise to deliver this mission. The meaning of the term "global," though, requires interrogation. What aspects of the education offered makes it global? Here I underscore three related meanings that "global" takes on in international schools run by TECs. The first is global as *homogenizing*. By this I mean that distinct spaces around the world are imagined as the same. The second meaning is global as *luxury consumption*. This notion of global is tied up with international education in English as an elite good, offered mostly in world financial and consumption centers. The third is global as *stratifying* in new ways. This meaning points to new forms of stratification, global or at least supranational in scale, which may emerge from international education.

Global as Homogenizing

Schools promise that their students will join an exclusive "global network" of students in the same school chain. GEMS Education, the largest transnational corporation that builds international schools, stresses its "Global GEMS school network of shared resources and learning." As the firm proclaims, "the global network of award winning GEMS schools aims to be a superior, lifelong collaborator in your child's education. Our students enjoy privileges like preferential placement in other GEMS schools, which enables a seamless GEMS education across the world" (GEMS website, http://gemschicagoearlyyears.com/why-a-gems-education/).

The same themes can be found in statements from other firms. Hong Kong-based Nord Anglia Education offers a "Global Classroom" program through which students in its various schools can connect. As Singapore's Dover Court International School, owned by Nord Anglia, announces, this program "unites our students with others around the world" (Nord Anglia). It goes on to note that: "As well as providing the community feel of a small school, we also benefit from the global learning collaborative of being part of a network of over 18,000 learners around the world" (Nord Anglia website, http://www.nordangliaeducation.com/our-schools/singapore/student-life/an-extended-global-family). The Global Indian International School (GIIS) states that "We encourage all our students to explore the world and its different cultures through our International Knowledge Exchange Programme. Our students get to interact in person with students and teachers from our global campuses through web-conferencing, thereby giving them an international outlook and satisfying their curiosity about new geographies" (Global Indian International School website, https://sg.globalindianschool.org/home/explore/global-knowledge-exchange).

This theme of global connection reaches its peak in the newest for-profit premier school chain, Avenues. The firm is preparing students for "global readiness." It is explicit in pointing out the merits of an integrated organization: "Think of Avenues as *one international school with 20 or more campuses.* It will not be a collection of 20 different schools all pursuing different educational strategies, but rather one highly-integrated 'learning community,' connected and supported by a common vision, a shared curriculum, collective professional development of its faculty, the wonders of modern technology and a highly-talented headquarters team" (Avenues website, https://www.avenues.org/en/the-world-school/). The Edison-founder and Avenue founder, Chris Whittle said, "The family is admitted not to the campus, but to the school as a whole" (*Education Investor*, December 14, 2011).

A global education can celebrate diversity. That is, the global might be a collection of various local places and their characteristics. But in most international school today, "global" is juxtaposed against "local." In portraying their schools as nodes in global corporate networks, school leaders also distance their institutions from local contexts. This distancing can be seen in the physical attributes of the schools. GEMS World Academy (GWA) Singapore, for example, is located in a neighborhood where a bustling public housing estate borders a country club-fringed reservoir. The site itself is a former golf course. The school's main gate opens to a street with heavy traffic and faces into the housing estate. This is a neighborhood made up of residents from all walks of life; hardly any family could afford GWA's enormous fees—and very few would hold the foreign citizenship needed for eligibility. Once in the school, though, you could not be further from this "heartlands" Singapore feeling. The walls are high and the security is formidable. In addition, precisely because the school is located in a heartlands neighborhood unlike the areas where students live, students have little contact with the world beyond the walls of their school. School buses take students straight to the on-site bus parking area; when they leave they simply hop on the bus again. This isolation makes it easier to imagine oneself connected to GWA students in Qatar or Chicago than to the students in the local school nearby.

The premium school chain Avenues appears to take pride in the separation of its schools from the neighborhoods in which they are located. Promotional material

The Meanings of a "Global" Education 93

juxtaposes the local orientation of old-fashioned schools with the global perspective of new schools: "Schools are historically rooted in the villages, towns and cities in which they are situated. Almost all are single-city, single-country institutions... Over time, some have evolved to serve 'national communities...' If 'local' schools are the first step in the evolution of schooling and "national" schools are the second step, the decades ahead are likely to bring the third step: *global schools*" (Avenues website, https://www.avenues.org/en/the-world-school/). The company places its own schools at the forefront of this support movement toward "global schools."

Global as Luxury Consumption

Layered on top of this homogenization is a treatment of international education as a consumer good. The homogenization of experiences in disparate places is a part of the spread of global consumer cultures. Sitting in a GWA school in one part of the world, one could be anywhere in the world. The same GEMS logo and slogans adorn the walls. The color schemes are familiar. The same "parent's café" can be found. Just like at a Starbucks outlet or an IKEA branch, one has the feeling of being nowhere rather than somewhere. The sameness of the designs and of what is on offer creates a feeling of connection to the brand that is removed from any local context. A particular school may offer a second language that is specific to the setting, but this is hardly a deviation: the IKEA café always has a local option alongside the meatballs.

Global as homogenization dovetails or underpins a particular sort of homogenization, one that resonates with consumer cultures. This twist on the meaning of "global" can be found in many casual discussions of globalization. Singapore, for example, is often said to be one of the most "globalized" places in the world. A stroll through town makes this assessment obvious: goods from all over the world are found in abundance. But this meaning of global is centered very much on the consumer. Another portrait of globalization would be across the Causeway in southern Malaysia, not fifteen minutes from Singapore. There one can find apartment towns, funded by Chinese developers, constructed by Indonesian and Bangladeshi workers, and purchased by Singapore residents. Another image still would be a factory town in rural India producing goods for export. The orders and prices they receive depend entirely on external markets. Are these places any less globalized than from a consumer's perspective? Clearly, "global" takes on distinct meanings because places sit in different parts of global networks. Imagining experiences as more or less global obscures qualitative distinctions in the ways a particular place is implicated in the global. It would be a very thin notion of global if we expected a highly-globalized world to look like Singapore.

TECs treat the global as the financial and consumption capitals of the world. Just as a luxury handbag brand may boast of their boutiques in world cities ("London—New York—Tokyo"), international school chains celebrate a similar collection of locations as "global." Global means being connected to this set of cities. Avenues is only the most obvious of the examples of this sort, with each of its schools located in or planned for one such global city. And with tuition set at close to USD 50,000 annually, there is no doubt that this is a luxury brand. There is good reason for this correspondence between this meaning of global and international school chains. International schools tend to be located in just such places, often serving the children of those employed in precisely those nodes of global capitalist networks. The families linked to international schools are generally already connected through work and consumption to these points in the world economy. Again, Avenues seeks to serve this mobility. It aspires to enable parents to send their children to the same schooling experience as they move from one global city to the next. The firm works closely with a property consultancy, CBRE, to identify and acquire property in such cities for establishing schools.

The claim that joining a chain of schools makes the education experience richer and more global is also striking. Certainly, parents can see the potential value in opportunities for students to interact with peers elsewhere in the world. Yet any school with Internet access and a few intrepid educators can achieve the same results. Schools need not belong to the same corporation in order to carry out exchanges. The practical value added here by the TEC is hard to see.[1] Perhaps, then, these organizations are advertising something more symbolic. What is offered is membership in a group defined by a corporation that claims to have certain status associations. Members of this group share affiliation with a particular brand. Members come from similarly high socioeconomic stations; students undertake similar courses of study. This version of being global is not about celebrating diversity or meeting people who are different from oneself. It is about connecting, at least in the imagination, with people are similar but who happen to sit in classrooms on different parts of the planet. Global consumer brands operate in similar fashion, creating and reflecting shared status for customers who are united by their belief in the social value of the product.

Global as Stratifying in New Ways

Since international schools target affluent families, a link between international schools and stratification is obvious. These schools are, in some ways, consequences of stratification. More than that, though, it may be the case that international school chains not only reflect stratification but also change it. While international schools have always served those who seek admission into leading universities often in their home areas, now they tend to serve anyone who seeks admission to these universities. Young people graduating from international schools may enter a transnational elite rather than a national one. In Asia, membership in a transnational elite distinguishes this generation from previous generations of elite. While national universities in East

---

[1] There is also reason to be suspicious of another advertised benefit of these chains—the claim that students can transfer seamlessly to another branch. The numbers of schools under one chain remain limited, so the likelihood that a move will take a family to city with an affiliated school may not be high. Moreover, many schools have waiting lists; allowing some to jump the queue would pose sensitive administrative problems.

The Meanings of a "Global" Education

Asia in particular have been core institutions of elite creation and perpetuation, international schools now serve as midway points to foreign universities appropriating those roles. A portion of the future elite in Asia is now getting a "global" education rather than a national one. They are gaining socialization experiences distinct from their compatriots and more similar to counterparts from other countries.

Certainly, having a section of the population with fluency in interacting with people of different national backgrounds is desirable. At best, this trend will create a cosmopolitanism that diminishes nationalist rivalry. But what loyalties will these young people have? Will they be oriented to their home countries (and families), or will this powerful socializing experience make them different? At worst, this trend can create a supranational elite with no political loyalties and few cultural affinities, except perhaps to a global consumer culture.

This form of stratification recalls colonialism. Under colonial rule, ambitious colonial subjects might, with some fortune, gain an education as designed by the colonizing power. Such an education would occur in the language of the empire and would involve socialization in the norms and values of the metropole. A bifurcation in the identities of those experiencing this type of education was the result. The metropole would never consider them equals, as they hailed from a colony, but after being socialized in a European or Japanese school, they would be unable to identify with their home culture either (Fanon, 1982). Some of the colonials educated this way would go on to serve as in leadership roles—to some, as "collaborators"—in their countries. The growth of strong national education systems, especially in East Asia, produced an alternative to the colonial model. Education was possible while retaining one's culture. That was the promise of nations, after all.

Today's globalization may involve elements of a return to the period before decolonization. Through international schools, elites are pulled out of their national systems and made different from the culture of their families. While it is too early to know what careers they will develop, we can speculate on the basis of the aspirations of their parents. The aim in attending international schools is to insert their children into the upper echelons of the global higher education hierarchy. Such status, in turn, is seen as a launching pad for a career that could occur in multiple parts of the world.

These notions of "global" can be contrasted with other ways of thinking about the mission of education. An alternative imagining of global can be seen in one international school group, United World College. A German educationist founded UWC in the 1960s on the philosophy that future world peace depends on young people of different countries talking to each other. He established a boarding school in Scotland for senior high school students from around the world. Branches of UWC were set up elsewhere—including in Singapore[2]—that followed the same pattern. The UWC vision was one where motivated teenagers from around the world would study together at one school. In other words, the global element occurred on the

---

[2]The Singapore branch, UWC Southeast Asia (UWCSEA), is unique among this family of schools for two reasons. First, its founders established it as a school mainly for expatriates rather than for boarders (it was originally called the Singapore International School). Second, UWCSEA runs education programs from nursery through secondary school.

school premises. This vision stands in stark contrast to that of the TECs, in which global community is created not through any single school but through belonging to a chain of schools. The "global networks" promised by the new TECs are not the only kind.

Another kind of contrast can be made. Many compulsory education systems in Western countries are built at least partly on the premise that education should be oriented to democratic citizenship. In the tradition of Dewey (2015), a purpose of schooling is to imbue in young people a sense of membership in a community of citizens. Students learn how to think critically about the world around them and how to engage in issues of significance to their community or country. With national borders erased from education, international schools can easily lose this democratic commitment. They can become especially susceptible to the corporate learning that has already infected public school systems, especially in the United States and United Kingdom, where for-profit schooling and private provision of pedagogical materials, socializes children into a world of exchange. International school chains, owned and operated by revenue-oriented organizations, tend to have a more corporate rather than democratic understanding of the mission of education. This point is true even though the content of what is conveyed in the classroom may stress global responsibilities and global citizenship. It is through the organization and social meaning of education that the corporate message is given.

International Education and Policy Networks

How do TECs advocate for their corporate-oriented ideas of global education? We can now examine the linkages between international school operators and influential actors. There are a number of ways that these businesses build connections with reputable public and international actors. These connections help in a variety of ways. They can be sources of insider information. They can help firms deal with rules from governments. They can lend legitimacy and credibility to education firms and their ideas. And they can work toward direct shifts in government policy. Some of these methods are done openly, in the name of public service, while others are quieter. Hiring staff from government or international organizations is one of the usually quieter ways.

The Revolving Door

Among the simplest ways that education firms insert themselves in global policy networks is through recruiting staff from government regulators or other education bodies (Verger et al., 2016: 155–156). There are numerous examples. People like Peter Birkett, for example, have been on both sides as an education businessman—holding his own education consultancy company, employee of a large education firm GEMS, and a national adviser of the UK. Zenna Atkins worked in the United Kingdom as chief of the Office of Education Standards (Ofsted), then shifted to GEMS (though she stayed on seven weeks). Figures such as these are active in the field. They support private companies' efforts to "make money from running state schools" (*Education Investor*, December 12, 2011).

The rotation of a set of experts between public and private roles can have a number of effects. It can provide firms with information on government that makes it easier to operate around regulations. Another way, when experts move in the opposite direction, is for regulation to be written in a way that might be more friendly to firms. In this capacity, they can change education law, diminish roles for government, and create opportunities for private businesses. The example of Anders Hultin demonstrates the movement of global experts in education. Hultin is a co-founder of Sweden's Kunskapsskolan, one of that country's largest private education providers. Upon completing his role with Kunskapsskolan, he moved to the UK and became an advocate for the free school policy in the UK. He could point to the Swedish example when to help make his case. He then went on to become the CEO of GEMS UK branch.

Another effect is to create a pool of experts who move between organizations but share a profession and a commitment to a certain approach to education. Zenna Atkins and Anders Hultin also argue that in order to make successful schools, providers should be allowed to make profit (*Education Investor*, December 12, 2011) They become advocates of a set of ideas, specifically for the idea that for-profit organizations should run schools. Experts also shift between schools. Peter Burdon, for example, worked as chief operating office at Nord Anglia from 2009 to 2013 before going on to become chief schools officer at GEMS. This flow of personnel may have some effect on anyone taking up positions in education administration. They are aware of opportunities for larger paychecks and status from the private sector.

Foundations and Charity Work

Through philanthropic activities, edu-businesses contribute to emerging forms of heterarchical education policymaking in which businesses, foundations, and international organizations, often connected through key individuals, shape effective policies. As recent research shows, philanthropy is a key means of education policymaking (Olmedo, 2014; Shamir, 2008; Srivastava, 2016). The Varkey Foundation, named after GEMS executive Sunny Varkey, partners with the Clinton Global Initiative. Bill Clinton is the honorary chairman of the foundation. The foundation's website displays a message from Bill Clinton, who is proud that Varkey Foundation is part of the Clinton Global Initiative community. Formed in 2010, the Foundation is best known for its Global Teacher Prize, a million-dollar award, which gets tremendous press coverage and which has branded itself as the "Nobel for education." Like the Gates Foundation and other business-friendly nonprofits, the Varkey Foundation identifies teacher quality rather than socioeconomic context as the challenge to improving education in poorer areas (Varkey Foundation website, https://www.varkeyfoundation. org/what-we-do/impact/). This activity also gives a leverage for them to be considered as the education expertise that can judge quality of education in the world.

The companies tend to use the name of founders of the education group, such as Varkey Foundation or Jeffrey Cheah Foundation. The goal of the Varkey Foundation is to "provide education to children who are in school ages in developing countries, but are not able to get education due to poverty, to train teachers, and to establish schools for developing countries." (Ibid.). In an interview, a representative explained that setting up a foundation was a business strategy for GEMS. It would be a way to show that the company cares about children and education beyond its immediate business activities.

A major approach of these foundations is to demonstrate that the organization has gained approval from world-renowned individuals. Take, for example, a promotional brochure from GEMS. The first and second pages of the brochure are taken up by a photograph of Bill Clinton and Varkey shaking hands. The first sentence of the brochure says that "GEMS Education is the first kindergarten to grade 12 education operator in the world to become a partner of the Clinton Global Initiative." Quotations from public figures adorn the brochure. They are from politicians, such as Tony Blair, former UK Prime Minister and Mark Vaile, former Deputy Prime Minister of Australia, to big corporations, such as Microsoft and LG Electronics, to educators, such as George Walker OBE former Director General of the International Baccalaureate Organization, and to Captain Barry E. "Butch" Wilmore NASA Astronaut and US Navy Pilot. Charity work helps firms reach out to public figures, then their endorsement becomes promotional material for the schools.

Global Education Experts

International organizations hold meetings on education with the participation of major education firms. For example, the International Finance Corporate (IFC), part of the World Bank Group, hosts the IFC Private Education Conference. There are also the International and Private Schools Education Forum, the Qatar Foundation's World Innovation Summit for Education (WISE), and the Global Education and Skills Forum (GESF). Many conferences and forums are invitation-only events or else have high registration fees. Furthermore, these events can be sponsored by corporate interests. GEMS Education established GESF. The company could foster in GESF an atmosphere of exclusivity and professionalism that improves the image of GEMS. The firm aims to have GESF to be considered "the Davos of Education" (Verger et al., 2016). Participants also build their own networks at these events. School operators may seek investors or look for investment and acquisition opportunities.

Government Consulting

Firms have also become involved in consulting for governments of countries in which they operate. Since 2014, for instance, Nord Anglia has run teacher training for government schools in Hong Kong. Sometimes, such work is done indirectly through consulting firms. These consulting firms, which make up the "consultocracy," can be more powerful or influential than elected democratic institutions (Verger et al., 2016: 150). These consultancies can be advocacy groups, such as School Choice Campaign, which advocated school choice and privatization in India or parent groups, such as the International Schools Parents Support Group (MISPSG) in Malaysia. This approach allows education firms to avoid taking public stances. They turn to loyal "experts" and outside organizations to make policy recommendations.

In other cases, private actors who do not directly work with TECs provide consulting on education reform. The Malaysian government invited the consulting firm McKinsey & Co to produce a 292-page proposal, the *Malaysian Education Blueprint, 2013–2025*. Francis Loh criticizes the government for paying RM20 million for this advice. McKinsey began giving education consulting in 2010 (Loh, 2014). While Loh points out that budget allocated to education is sufficient—Malaysia's basic education expenditure as a percentage of GDP is higher than OECD average—the problem is distribution. Due to poor budget allocation, improving the quality of education and training teachers are difficult tasks. Loh supports the *Blueprint's* point that education should be decentralized. However, the former emphasizes that decentralization should be led by teachers and schools. The latter recommends the private sector to take a major role. Most relevant here, the *Blueprint* suggests scaling up international schools as a priority for Malaysian education policy (Malaysia Education Blueprint, 2013: 207). Only three years after the McKinsey report, Malaysia's policies welcomed international schools, as we saw in Chap. 3.

As these examples indicate, firms in international education are well-linked in global education policy networks. They draw legitimacy from prestigious institutions and actors, including both private and public ones. This discussion points to broader themes of how power operates in global affairs. In particular, we see how firms active in a new, narrow economic field can link themselves into established international institutions and tap into the reputations of respected individuals and organizations. They can then mobilize these links to lobby for their own, corporatized notions of education. They can play dual roles as public and private actors. On one hand, as operators, they can claim to just be businesses seeking a profit and able to use any legal means to do so. On the other hand, through charities they claim space in public discussions of how education ought to operate. That public work then feeds into promotional work for the private business.

Conclusion

Firms operating in the field of international education are enmeshed in global education policy networks. They take public positions, and they gain prestige and influence through their activities and their associations with respected international organizations and individuals. Three main conclusions follow.

First, these firms and their allies advocate a particular vision of "global" education, one that is distinct from other possible visions. The promise of making our children prepared for a "global" life is rightly enticing, but critical investigation is crucial to reflect on what this means. By stressing a homogeneity across space, TECs overlook local differences and view the global in juxtaposition to the local rather than as an amalgam. International school chains also present the "global" as luxury consumption. The vision is also one of stratification. This is a corporate-friendly notion of global. It is like a high-status brand, whose meaning is "read" by those of the "right" social class in different parts of the world. Moreover, it creates economies of scale, across national boundaries, which are appealing to transnational firms. These firms have in turn depended on other forces and actors like IB and university rankings that denationalize education. This vision of "global" is different from one that celebrates diversity. It also does not put the stress on a "democratic" education.

Second, firms propagate their idea of "global" education, and their preferred policies, by drawing on the prestige of international actors. This gives legitimacy to their organizations and goals, and helps to further their interests. These interests are most especially in international schools but are not confined to that: they are also in schooling for the poor in the developing world, in early education, and in school systems (through advising). These activities challenge the state as an education policy actor. This role is one of the main reasons why education transnationals deserve our attention. International education may seem remote from the concerns of most families and educators, but it is one space where private actors are growing, building resources, and generating respectability.

Third, and finally, the experience of TECs illustrates a dimension of global governance more broadly. In a quiet, seemingly innocuous corner, actors can chip away at accountable state power. In this case, a new set of firms emerged in a niche area, and have now become players that actively attempt to shape global ideas and agendas. This power feeds into the aspirations of many people, especially Asia's upwardly mobile. Global governance in this sphere works by shaping people's aspirations, building support for changes in government policy. It is not so much that state power is directly eroded, but—as seen in Chaps. 4 and 5—states can be brought into support corporatized international education. Then, the ability of communities and citizens to protect their education systems can be diminished.

Where does this critical assessment leave us in thinking about international education? Scrutiny of these firms is in itself a value, especially in this case. TECs, because they operate in an area where people are not especially vulnerable and across national boundaries, have been subject to scant public scrutiny. Discussing their activities is a first step toward regaining some accountability. It is also valuable,

Conclusion

though, to think about steps toward responding to this new type of actor and thinking about what "global" or "international" education should mean. I take this task up in the Conclusion.

References

Avenues website. *The World School*. https://www.avenues.org/en/the-world-school/. Accessed January, 2018.
Ball, S. J. (2012). *Global Education Inc.: New policy networks and the neo-liberal imaginary*. New York: Routledge.
Dewey, J. (2015). *Democracy and education, an introduction to the philosophy of education*. CreateSpace Independent Publishing Platform.
Education Investor. (2011, December 12). Interviewing Zenna Atkins.
Education Investor. (2011, December 14). City Slickers.
Fanon, F. (1982). *Black skin, white masks*. (C. L. Markmann, Trans.). New York: Grove Press.
GEMS website. *Why a GEMS education*. http://gemschicagoearlyyears.com/why-a-gems-education/. Accessed January, 2018.
GIIS (Global Indian International School) website. *Global knowledge exchange*. https://sg.globalindianschool.org/home/explore/global-knowledge-exchange. Accessed January, 2018.
Gulson, K. N., & Lubienski, C. (2014). The new political economy of education policy: Cultural politics, mobility and the market: A response to M. Peters' 'four contexts for philosophy of education and its relation to education policy'. *Knowledge Cultures, 2*(2), 70–79.
Loh, F. (2014). Malaysia's education system in crisis? *Aliran Monthly, 33*(8).
Malaysia Education Blueprint 2013–2025. (2013). *Ministry of Education*. http://planipolis.iiep.unesco.org/sites/planipolis/files/ressources/malaysia_blueprint.pdf. Accessed August–September, 2017.
MTI (Ministry of Trade and Industry Singapore). (2012, October 19). *Speech by Mr. Teo Ser Luck, Minister of State for Trade and Industry, at the Stamford American International School Campus Opening Ceremony*. https://www.mti.gov.sg/NewsRoom/Pages/Mr-Teo-Ser-Luck-at-the-Stamford-American-International-School-Campus-Opening-Ceremony.aspx. Accessed August 1, 2018.
Nord Anglia website. http://www.nordangliaeducation.com/our-schools/singapore/student-life/an-extended-global-family. Accessed January, 2018.
Olmedo, A. (2014). From England with love… ARK, heterarchies and global 'philanthropic governance'. *Journal of Education Policy, 29*(5), 575–597.
Robertson, S. L. & Verger, A. (2012). Governing education through public private partnerships. *Centre for Globalisation, Education and Societies*. University of Bristol. https://susanleerobertson.files.wordpress.com/2012/07/2012-robertson-verger-governing-education.pdf. Accessed May, 2018.
Shamir, R. (2008). The age of responsabilization: On market-embedded morality. *Economy and Society, 37*(1), 1–19.
Spring, J. (2015). *Economization of Education: Human capital, global corporations, skill-based schooling*. New York: Routledge.
Srivastava, P. (2016). Philanthropic engagement in education. *Contemporary Education Dialogue, 13*(1), 5–32.
Varkey Foundation website. *What we do*. https://www.varkeyfoundation.org/what-we-do/impact/. Accessed January, 2018.
Verger, A., Fontdevila, C., & Zancajo, A. (2016). *The privatization of education: A political economy of global education reform*. New York: Teachers College Press.

World Bank. (2011). *Learning for all: investing in people's knowledge and skills to promote development—World Bank Group education strategy 2020*. Washington, DC: World Bank. http://documents.worldbank.org/curated/en/169531468331015171/Learning-for-all-investing-in-peoples-knowledge-and-skills-to-promote-development-World-Bank-Group-education-strategy-2020. Accessed July, 2018.

Chapter 8
Conclusion

Many international schools avoid the problems I have described. Commercial interests do not drive all of the schools, and do not drive all aspects of any of them. Schools that teach in a language other than English are also freer from corporatizing influence. These schools tend to be less closely linked to global education hierarchies, and therefore of less interest to edu-businesses. None of the points made here are meant as arguments against private education, against international schools, or even against for-profit schooling. Rather, I have pointed to a potentially troubling trend in which international school incorporation into transnational businesses contributes to the wealth and prominence of those firms and challenges the integrity of public education systems. Concern with this trend is separate from any judgments about international schools or private schools more broadly.

Making Education Global

Chapter 6 pointed to the corporate, and even quasi-imperialist, meanings of "global" that have snuck into international education. As educators, parents, and citizens, we should demand higher standards in thinking about the global in education. Global need not mean homogenizing experiences across space. Airports or chain stores are not the best models of global. Giving young people an understanding of their locality's place in the broader world is important, and it draws attention to diversity rather than uniformity in the world.

The aspiration for global education is an admirable one. Cultivating awareness of our place in the wider world and building appreciation for different cultures are important educational goals. Corporatized international schools seize on important themes. Many of the slogans are good: global citizenship, holistic learning, and so forth. The problem is that they are slogans. That is, these ideas are turned into devices for marketing. In real-world contexts, this practical purpose re-figures the

© The Author(s), under exclusive license to Springer Nature Singapore Pte Ltd., part of Springer Nature 2019
H. Kim, *How Global Capital is Remaking International Education*, SpringerBriefs in Education, https://doi.org/10.1007/978-981-32-9672-5_8

stated mission. The main challenge here is that the way education is organized and delivered affects what global comes to mean in practice.

Good ideas end up being used to reinforce hierarchies. "Global citizenship" comes to be a marker of distinction. "Holistic learning" can end up feeding into cram school economies, because parents in some contexts see the value of an IB degree in a particular way, even though the IB philosophy stands in direct opposition to the cram school approach. Learning English can widen young people's horizons, but many families pursue English-language education so that children can scale Western-centric hierarchies. Because corporatized international schools are tied up in purposes of generating revenue and appealing to families that define their ambitions in a particular way, these schools are inherently limited in delivering the types of pedagogies they process. Recognizing this limit is important, especially in a world where firms are regarded as models for human organization.

Implications for Teaching and Learning

What do these commercial tendencies mean for teaching and learning in international schools? While a full treatment of this question is beyond the scope of this book, a few comments are in order. Many schools that have the backing of transnational education corporations have impressive resources to put toward educating their pupils. At least a portion of these resources do work toward improving the quality of teaching. As any educator knows, financial backing can make a big difference in attempting to build exciting education programs. Student-teacher ratios can be brought down, more ambitious projects can be undertaken, and libraries can be expanded.

International schools risk missing the opportunities to establish and promulgate exciting visions of international or global education. These schools could emerge as leaders in innovating techniques in international education. We have international schools of unprecedented wealth and ambitious, and they could be sources of new ways of undertaking international education. Those techniques might be disseminated to other schools, where they could benefit many more students.

Over and over again, however, I have observed schools not grappling with central questions in international education. Take, for example, history and social studies. Whose history should be taught in an international school with no national affiliation? This question is a complex one, with multiple possible answers. In national or public schools, the starting point for studying history is clear—and socializing children in ways of thinking about the nation has long been a central component of national education. As international schools have become unhinged from national curricula, the answer is far less obvious. Studying the history of the host nation is one option, but many schools and their students are disconnected from the host society. There is an opportunity to develop interesting criteria that imagine the school's location in space and time in new ways. Yet there is little evidence that schools are taking this opportunity. Instead, school after school opts for similar "global" histories.

Implications for Teaching and Learning 105

The problem is that the pressure of marketing drives so much of what happens in these schools. Schools devote their energies to recruitment, to sending signals to parent-consumers. This mode of engagement leaves little space for careful crafting of curricula. As noted for other contexts, market competition in education does not necessarily produce variety and expanded "choice." Instead of seeing elite international schools developing fascinating curricula that might inspire others with fewer resources, they stick to a common model. Following the logic of economization, differences are imagined more in terms of quality—results for cost—than variety.

The State and Education

These points underscore the limits of corporatized education. Just as distressing, though, is that the state's role in education is shifting away from providing and overseeing school systems to subordinating education to economic policy. The state's role is shifting toward that of the "competition state," as other education researchers have pointed out. Chapter 5 showed how state aims of raising national economic competitiveness led to support for international school businesses that, in turn, may threaten the integrity of education systems. If education policy is merely an extension of economic policy, then education systems will be in trouble.

Citizens should question governments that cite economic competition as reason for supporting education businesses. Where transnational education corporations (TECs) gain tax breaks and discounted access to property, in the name of contributing to competitiveness, questions need to be raised. These measures, while appearing minor, cut to core issues of what the state's purpose is. Is the state's purpose simply to make decisions that might raise GDP? Or do these concerns need to be weighed against values of fairness and goals of creating inclusive, accessible education systems?

Education corporations have not yet ignited debate in Asian societies over education privatization. Perhaps such debate is coming. Instead of starting an open debate, though, edu-businesses have amassed wealth, connections, and prestige. When and where any debate opens, it will not be merely a conversation. TECs will have tremendous resources to throw behind their positions. They will have the support of the wealthier and more influential elements in society, who may have already opted out of public systems. And they will appeal to symbols and ideals that they have already implanted in public imaginaries. While public education systems appear robust in parts of the region, an array of corporate forces are quietly and rapidly growing in strength.

The treatment of corporatized international schools as models for education should also be a concern. These schools may have many impressive features. Their budgets may allow them to introduce wonderful technologies to students and their connections to international institutions may create special opportunities for young people. But these schools do not play by the same rules. They are not embedded in a system of accountability. Schools that are not part of a system by definition do not have the same responsibilities. They do not have to worry about inclusivity and reaching all of society. An education system is defined first of all by its social purpose. Any accomplishments in schools within a public education system comes within a context where certain principles must be upheld. Corporatized international schools do not have these constraints precisely because they do not have the same social purpose. We cannot use the same standards to judge a school that is outside that system as we would judge schools within the system. This logic, so common in many fields today, is simply incorrect.

It should, therefore, ring hollow when governments and international organizations turn to edu-businesses for advice and partnership. Public officials should exercise restraint when lending prestige to these for-profit bodies. If governments solicit advice from TECs, then they should be aware that they are lending status to for-profit actors who have no record of providing public services. Agencies at the United Nations should consider the implications of privileging elite school chains when forming partnerships. News agencies also have roles to play. Media organizations should consider carefully when they report positively on the philanthropic activities of edu-businesses. These activities are public relations initiatives: if nobody heard about them, then they would have no impact on public thinking, so if the media ignores them, then they will have less influence. By treating discussions among wealthy people—such as at Davos—as news, media put such people into the forefront of public debate.

Not only in education, but in other fields, too, the firm has become a model for how the state should operate. The "new public management" school of thought encouraged government leaders to believe that firms are more efficient and, therefore, state services should be out-sourced to private interests. As Crouch (2000) observes in his book, *Coping with Post-Democracy*, holding up the firm as a model undermines democratic principles. Firms can avoid issues of accountability. To the extent that states shift public activities to unaccountable bodies, citizens lose power. The growth of transnational edu-business threatens to bring this effect into education systems, especially in Asia. As these firms gain wealth, prestige, and credit for their "expertise," and as states subordinate education to economic imperatives, public accountability in education may slip away. Shedding light on these subtle forms of politics is important for forestalling that prospect.

Reference

Crouch, C. (2000). *Coping with post-democracy*. London: Fabian Society.

Printed in the United States
By Bookmasters